BOB MARLEY:

BOB MARLEY
A Life

Garry Steckles

Interlink Books

An imprint of Interlink Publishing Group, Inc.
Northampton, Massachusetts

This edition published in 2021 by

INTERLINK BOOKS
An imprint of Interlink Publishing Group, Inc.
46 Crosby Street, Northampton Massachusetts 01060
www.interlinkbooks.com

Library of Congress Cataloging-in-Publication Data
Steckles, Garry.
 Bob Marley : a life / by Garry Steckles.—1st American ed.
   p. cm.
Includes bibliographical references and index.
ISBN 978-1-56656-733-6 (pbk.)
1. Marley, Bob. 2. Reggae musicians—Jamaica—Biography. I. Title.
ML420.M3313S74 2008
782.421646092—dc22   [B]

                        2008023775

Printed and bound in the United States of America

To request our complete 40-page full-color catalog, please call us toll free at
1-800-238-LINK, visit our website at www.interlinkbooks.com, or write to
Interlink Publishing, 46 Crosby Street, Northampton, MA 01060
email: info@interlink books.com

Contents

Livicated to the memory of:

Ashok Chandwani
Charles B. Comer
Valerie Cowan
Joseph Hill
St Clair "Sint" Illidge
Bevin Jackson
Tony Johnson
Peter McIntosh
Robert 'Scotty' Osborne

Good friends we have lost, along the way

Miss Cedella's Son   David Michael Rudder

Every time I hear that raspy voice, and those songs. Oh those songs!
Man I'm so proud that my life is touched by your raw Caribbean soul
And we're still hypnotized by the vibe of the 'Toughest Gong'
Near and far, from lands in the sun to the lands of the cold
Congo bongo man, reaching way beyond Seventh Street
In a rub-a-dub style, your roots reggae really rocked the planet
Pure and simple, yet sophisticated and oh so sweet
All could feel our Caribbean energy, reconfirmed every time you jam it
The thirsty were quenched, the hot got cool, as you stirred it up . . . stiff
Emancipating us in every strum, until it felt like the cold four hundred
　　　years just faded with every riff

Yaggo Yo! Ride, Natty, ride. Wo-yoh yoh yoh
Onto our consciousness, Miss Cedella, was born your son
U and you alone know what you do and what you go through
Rising through sufferers' nights to an ever-liberating dawn
Songs of freedom, songs of love eternal
Eternally living through every generation's dawning
Living in the dreams that dance in every sufferer's bed
Freedom in the misty morning

Freedom in the St. Ann's hills, Trench Town, and the Dungle
Roots to rock the motherland, and the concrete jungle
One love, one heart, this Wailer connection
Music, our music, as the seed of correction

Musician, mystic, wailing soul
Every man's cry coming from a grounded voice
Naked truths and firm beliefs, hope and heartache
Truth is truth, and there's no choice
All aboard the Zion train, where every song is a station
Leading us away from a dread situation

Sun is still shining, weather still sweet though
Liberation oozes from every drum and every bass
All in all, we've done well with the cards we've been dealt
Verily verily, in the end, we'll truly find our place
Every time I hear that relentless strum, I know you're still on the job
Reminding us of the work to be done
Yes man, you're still walking good Mr. Bob, Miss Cedella's son.

INTRODUCTION
So Dem Seh

A Bob Marley comes along perhaps once in a lifetime—and then only if you're lucky enough to be born in roughly the same era as him, a millisecond in the story of our planet. Of all the great Caribbean lives we've been privileged to see and be part of—this is a small corner of the earth, and its great people tend not to be remote from its common folk—Nesta Robert Marley's is truly special.

His quantifiable achievements are impressive. The record attendances at his live performances. The recognition of *Exodus*, by *Time* magazine, as the finest album ever recorded. The United Nations Peace Medal, awarded to Bob on behalf of all Africans. The tens of millions of albums sold since he left us, bodily, in 1981. The choice of "One Love" by the British Broadcasting Corporation as the anthem to close the twentieth century. The time capsule buried by the *New York Times*, not to be unearthed until the end of this millennium, containing a Bob Marley concert video as the outstanding example of popular culture in our times. The induction to the Rock and Roll Hall of Fame. The Lifetime Achievement Grammy.

All very impressive, all thoroughly well deserved.

But the true measure of Bob Marley's greatness isn't nearly so tangible. It can be found in the far-flung corners of the earth, places many of us have barely heard of but where Bob Marley's name, Bob Marley's music, and Bob Marley's message bring joy and inspiration to the lives of millions.

His image—on hats, shoes, postcards, bumper stickers, postage stamps, coins, belts, tattoos, and countless millions of T-shirts—is everywhere. So is his music. Collectively, many of us were blessed that our trod on this troubled planet coincided with his. And we've done a pretty good job of making sure that those born since Bob left us have shared this blessing, by exposing them to his music, by listening to what he taught us and by doing our best to live the way Bob would have wanted us to.

Culled from a variety of sources—with particular thanks to the annual Marley Collectors' Edition of *The Beat* magazine—the quotes that follow give a far better idea than any formal accolades of what Bob Marley means to the world.

Bob Marley is not even about knowledge any more, Bob Marley is a way of life. Bob Marley is like the soundtrack of the existence today in Africa. Bob's music is beyond the century. Bob's music was part of God, and God is timeless. It expressed God's being in sound and words, so it's timeless. It's part of us, part of our being.

—Rocky Dawuni, reggae singer-songwriter, *Ghana*

Bob has changed my life for the best. He taught me we are all one people, whatever colour or race we are, in the eyes of the Almighty God. He has continuously inspired me and given me strength. I give thanks and praise for the message he shared with us through his music.

—Isaac Haile Selassie, musician, Los Angeles (originally from Ethiopia, where he was one of many orphans adopted by Emperor Haile Selassie I)

Bob Marley acted, and acts, as a reminder to us of something that we all have deeply embedded in our spirits, that of truth, honesty, and love.

—Matt Jenson, music teacher, Boston

Nepalese people embraced Bob into their souls through his music and Rasta beliefs. After all, "rasta" in Hindi means a path, a roadway, mostly of the spiritual journey. To this day, Bob is worshipped in Nepal as an ascetic, as a holy man, as an incarnation of Vishnu. His music will live forever.

—Sanjay Dev, Katmandu, Nepal and Chico, California

He came with pure words, no violence, no nothing. Pure words that you could listen to and educate yourself from.

—Tappa Zukie, musician, Jamaica

As a native American, you become familiar with the rhythms of Bob Marley, as every other car that goes by has his songs blaring from their speakers. I was in a store here some time back, wearing a Bob Marley T-shirt, and a small boy not more than five years old, noticing my shirt, immediately broke into his version of "Buffalo Soldier."
　　　　　　　　　　—JoAnn P. Thorne, Peridot, Arizona

In Nicaragua during the war against the Contras in the 1980s, you would find Sandinista soldiers singing Bob Marley songs, singing "Road Block." Then, when we visited the Contra camps, you would find the Contra people singing Bob's songs.
　　　　　　　　　　　　—Dr. Gail McGarrity, Jamaica

In 2096, when the former Third World has overrun and colonized the former superpowers, Bob Marley will be commemorated as a saint.
　　　　　　—Jon Pareles, pop music critic, *New York Times*

Throughout history great people have touched this world. But only Bob Marley has transcended into a space that appears to have no limit on time. He is my teacher of good will and rebellion. His work is truly a blessing for all of us to share.
　　　　—Mark Moses Alvarado, radio disc jockey and social worker

In the two decades since Bob Marley has gone, it is clear that he is without question one of the most transcendent figures of the past hundred years. The ripples of his unparalleled achievements radiate outward through the river of his music into an ocean of politics, ethics, fashion, philosophy and religion. His story is a timeless myth made manifest in this Iwah, right before our disbelieving eyes.
—Roger Steffens, author, broadcaster, musicologist, Marley historian and founder/curator of the Reggae Archives in Los Angeles

There's something about him that is unexplainable. He was sent here by God himself to perform a work.
　　　　　　—Tony Chin, Jamaican guitarist, who has played on
　　　　　　　　　　hundreds of classic reggae recordings

His songs will be hymns and anthems that people can use to build a new world. He had a vision like Martin Luther King and Coltrane of a world with no flags, no borders, no money.
                    —Carlos Santana, legendary guitarist

I meet a lot of people on the road, and they come to me and say if it wasn't for your dad they'd probably be dead...probably committed suicide. I have grown men break down cryin', literally cryin' and huggin' me, and letting me know it's my dad that saved their life, even though they never met my dad. It is very inspiring to know what is done strictly through music.
                —Ky-Mani Marley, recording artist and Bob Marley's
                                          second-youngest son

I travel to Asia a lot on business, and when I'm in a country like China, or India, or Bali and I tell people I'm from St. Kitts they haven't a clue where I'm talking about. Then I say the Caribbean, and they still haven't a clue. Then I say Bob Marley—and without fail, their faces light up with recognition.
—Maurice Widdowson, businessman, St. Kitts, Eastern Caribbean

Bob is somebody who was an incredible role model. Anybody you talk to, who has witnessed him, knows he really led by example. He was always on time for things, which is hardly a Jamaican trait. I went on a lot of the 1980 tour and he was always the first one on the bus. Traditionally, the star is the last one on the bus, if he isn't going in a limo. If there were a lot of people and they had to fly economy, he would travel with them. He never put himself in a position where he would be seen as different than anyone else. In that respect, he was someone who lived up to the example of the leaders of all the main religions: there is one quality all such figures have, which is humility. And Bob really had that quality.
                    —Chris Blackwell, founder of Island Records

Bob Marley's music was about reality, a dread reality. His Jamaican experience gave him insight into the human condition in ways that he could speak to everyone, and it was as if the people to whom he spoke

*were ready for that message. The natural mystic had indeed arrived.
On a personal level he was just a great brother to be around, and I miss
him greatly. Michael Manley once said of him that a great artist moves
from passion to compassion. Indeed, that is why he wrote such great
love songs, for, as he said, he had to, and as a youth he was made much
of by the women around him in Nine Mile, but also he had, as he said,
the blessings of women, and he drew the example of how he once saw a
woman falling down and he rushed to her rescue and eased her down,
breaking her fall. She told him: "God bless you, mi son." Bob said it was
those blessings he had, and that they could not be taken away.*

—Dermott Hussey, Jamaican broadcaster, writer and co-author,
with Malika Lee-Whitney, of *Bob Marley:
Reggae King of the World*

*He is not gone, man, his work is here. He is alive. Whenever you call
his name, you bring him alive. The reservoir of music he left behind
him is like an encyclopedia; when you need to refer to a certain situation or crisis, there will always be a Bob Marley song that will relate
to it. Bob was a musical prophet. I've gotten to realize, in reading my
Bibles, that this man was really Joseph in his second advent.*

—Judy Mowatt, member of I-Three, who toured and recorded
with Bob 1974–80

*He was ordained from he was born to be a king—in music, soccer,
whatever. But God gave him music and he went and he delivered. He's
like a young prophet. It was good for me to live with him and eat with
him, drink with him and smoke with him...I can lift my hat to the
king Marley. I tell you, man, I just love him. I mean, without any
apology. I'll cry for Bob. I'll do anything for Bob.*

—Antonio "Gilly" Gilbert, Bob's cook on the road 1976–80

*One dramatic story of a Marley "sighting" comes from a Cambridge
professor who visited Tibet in 1979 after it had been closed for decades
of Chinese occupation. At the Potola lamasert in Lhasa, an ageing
monk led the visitor through underground catacombs into a room
carved out of rock, where a single light bulb and an old eight-track tape*

player were plugged into a single electric outlet. In the tape player a Lebanese bootleg of Natty Dread *played over and over.*

—From the book *On Racial Frontiers: The New Culture of Frederick Douglass, Ralph Ellison and Bob Marley* by Gregory Stephens, scholar, author and Marley fan

I was traveling in Sudan in 1980, clinging to the top of a truck on the road from Khartoum to Juba. The only person we saw in hours was a tribesman in the distance, holding a boom box to his ear. When we got closer I heard what he was listening to: Bob Marley, singing "No Woman No Cry."

—Lucinda Chodan, editor in chief, *Victoria Times Colonist,* British Columbia, Canada

I think he's one of the true, true, heroes. Of oppressed people, of people who come from nothing and so they're treated like nothing. I think he's right up there with Martin Luther King and John F. Kennedy, anybody who devoted their life to protecting the lives of people, God-given rights to a decent life, a wholesome life, and a life that has opportunity for whatever it is you want to achieve.

—Cindy Breakspeare, former Miss World and mother of Damian "Junior Gong" Marley

From the purity of young romance, to the uncompromising commitment of revolution, and every emotion in between, no voice has ever spoken such transcendent truth with such authority and communicated it so effectively. It will be many generations before music again produces an artist so respected and beloved worldwide as Bob Marley.

—Steven "Little Steve" Van Zandt, guitarist with Bruce Springsteen's E-Street Band and star of the TV series *The Sopranos*

Bob Marley's music acts as our guide to a correct and positive way of life, leading and reassuring us all the way. His messages chronicle every foreseeable situation, problem, pressure and emotion, offering us lessons in handling these life experiences. By continually drawing from the everflowing wisdom found in his songs, we are able to overcome any roadblock and all struggles fade away. The daily goal of painting positivity in all aspects of life is one of the greatest treasures we find in Bob's music. Bob Marley's messages were always succinct and expressed in a heartfelt package that nourish our souls. Always 100 percent natural. Always pure positivity.

—Seth and Daniel Nelson, reggae webmasters (Iration.com) and Marley devotees

And to think I knew that man.

—Neville Willoughby, legendary Jamaican broadcaster

Home to rest: Bob's mausoleum at Nine Mile. To the right, the humble wooden home he lived in with his mother in the late forties and returned to with Rita in 1967.

1.

Birth of a Legend

Events of significance that took place on 6 February 1945:

• In Yalta, a resort town on the Crimean Riviera, Allied leaders Franklin D. Roosevelt of the United States, Winston Churchill of Great Britain, and Joseph Stalin of the Soviet Union met to plan the final defeat and occupation of Nazi Germany and how they'd carve up Europe as the end of the Second World War drew close.

• In Germany, the Red Army crossed the River Oder, putting it within fifty miles of the German capital of Berlin and the bunker in which Adolf Hitler was waiting out the last days of the war.

• In Nine Mile, deep in the heart of rural Jamaica, a baby was born.

There was nothing—not a barely-heard fanfare of rassbrass trumpets, not the distant echo of a nyabhingi drum, not so much as a bass-like rumble of thunder—to let the world know the infant who'd just been born was going to influence and change the lives of tens of millions of people, that his face would become the best-known in the history of mankind, that the music he would make and the message it would carry would penetrate the consciousness of far-flung corners of the planet, that his melodies would make us dance while his lyrics were making us think, that he would spread wisdom and joy around the earth in equal measure.

The birth of Nesta Robert Marley wasn't exactly run of the mill, however.

1

For one thing, his father was a white man. For another, he was an old white man—and the baby's mother was the teenage daughter of the most important and respected man in the tightly knit, deeply religious, highly traditional, and totally black community of Nine Mile, nestled in the Rhoden Hall district in the lush hinterland of Jamaica's "garden parish" of St. Ann.

Cedella Marley was the sixth of nine children of Omeriah Malcolm and his wife Alberta Wilbey. The nine, by all accounts, were only a fraction of the number Omeriah fathered by various women in the district, among them a further nine by three sisters. He had a seemingly boundless enthusiasm for procreation that would soon be passed on to his grandson.

The long-suffering, stoical Alberta died when Cedella was only ten, and from then the bright and occasionally feisty young girl was raised by Omeriah and her oldest sister, Enid.

Omeriah, a well-to-do man, was a farmer, and a proud one, and when she wasn't at school Cedella loved to help cultivate his yams, sweet potatoes, cassava, and corn and tend to his pigs, goats, and chickens.

When the sun had set over Nine Mile, and the languid night air was filled with the tropical evening sound of whistling tree frogs, it was usually time for music. It was always live music—electricity hadn't reached rural Jamaica in those days. Omeriah himself played the accordion and the violin, and another relative was an accomplished, semi-professional musician who played banjo, violin, and guitar in one of the mento-quadrille bands that provided the entertainment at local social gatherings, performing popular melodies in a uniquely Jamaican style, not unlike early calypso, that had evolved from both the musicians' African roots and the music that had been favored by the island's European elite in the mid-nineteenth century. The influence of mento was to surface, many years later, in Bob Marley's first recording, "Judge Not."

Cedella, who had inherited a fine voice from her mother, loved music from her earliest days, and was soon singing gospel with the choir of the Shiloh Apostolic Church in the nearby village of Eight Mile, Alberta's birthplace.

The young Cedella attended school at Stepney, which was miles away from her home and which she had to walk to and from every day. There, she encountered the sort of harsh discipline that was the norm at Caribbean schools in those days—and, sadly, still is at many—consisting, usually, of the administration of vicious "licks" for the most trivial of perceived transgressions.

She also had a temper when crossed—a trait Nesta would inherit from her and which would eventually help him survive in the streets and alleys of Trench Town and the shark-infested waters of the music business. At ten, not long after the death of her mother, Cedella went to the aid of her sister Amy, who was being bullied by a gang of older boys from their school. She rushed to her sister's side, picking up a stone, throwing it into the face of the tormentors' ringleader and, as she puts it, "busting his head."

She emerged from that skirmish victorious, but a few days later she learned that the gang members were out for revenge and planned to ambush her during her long trek to school. She begged Omeriah to let her stay home and help him in his fields, which was how she preferred to spend her days anyhow. He agreed—and from then on her daily trek wasn't to Stepney and the hated school, but to Omeriah's fields in Smith, about three miles from Nine Mile. There, she helped with the planting and with preparing the daily meal for her father's workers, all ravenous after spending hours toiling on the land.

This timeless rural cycle became Cedella's daily life, and she continued to make the regular trip from Nine Mile to Smith as she reached her early teenage years.

It was during these uneventful daily treks that Cedella started to take notice of something highly unusual—something that would soon change her life, forever.

A white man. To be more specific, a white man on a horse.

Captain Norval Marley was a quartermaster attached to the British West Indian Regiment. He was a member of an old white Jamaican family, and had just been appointed overseer of Crown land in the district of Rhoden Hall. Captain Marley soon befriended Omeriah Malcolm, and, before long, he'd become a regular visitor to the family's home.

Despite their considerable age difference—he was about fifty, she was in her early to mid-teens—the white overseer soon started showing a less than platonic interest in young Cedella. At first, she was afraid, running to hide whenever she saw him riding towards the house.

Eventually, with her sixteenth birthday behind her, the captain's sometimes crude advances started to interest her rather than scare her into hiding.

By now, Norval Marley had moved into a house nearby that he was renting from Cedella's grandmother, Yaya. He was always asking young Cedella to visit him, and it was obvious he had other things on his mind than chatting about the weather and catching up on local labberish. At first, she teased and frustrated him, telling him yes and meaning no. Then, late one night, her teenage curiosity and yearnings overcoming her better judgement, she decided to visit the persistent and by now strangely attractive white man. She quietly left Omeriah's house, cautiously made her way up the nearby hill to the captain's rented home, and stayed with him until early morning, when she sneaked back into her own bed.

It was the first time Cedella Marley had been with a man.

She felt a genuine warmth for the captain—a warmth that never diminished, despite the callous way he would eventually treat her and her son—and the nocturnal visits continued, unchecked, until a fateful evening when one of her brothers, who was sharing her room, woke up and noticed something was missing: his sister. He roused their sleeping father, and, after scouring the house for the absent girl, it dawned on Omeriah and Enid—who had seen Cedella exchange a wink with Marley a few days previously—that, in Enid's words, "she could be over at Captain's."

Within minutes, Omeriah was hammering on the door of Yaya's small wooden house—where his teenage daughter and the fifty-something white man he considered his good friend had been fast asleep in the same bed.

Unable to face the wrath of her father, a terrified Cedella quickly decided there was only one thing she could do—flee. She managed to elude the angry Omeriah, and this time, instead of quietly picking her way down the familiar hill, she practically flew down it, dashing into the house to grab a bag she kept in her room and then hiding in the cellar, barely daring to breathe.

When the hubbub had died down, and Omeriah had retired to bed, uttering dire threats of what would happen when he caught up with his wayward daughter the next morning, Cedella managed to sneak out of the cellar and headed out into the dead of night.

Walking for miles every day had been part of her life for as long as she could remember, and hours later Cedella arrived at the home, in Alva, of Alberta's father, Uncle Dan—her grandfather. He let her stay with him, but after she'd been there for less than a week the captain, who'd learned where she was hiding, rode up to the house and tearfully begged her to return home, pleading that her outraged father was threatening to take him to court.

She refused, and kept on refusing, until eventually she agreed it was time for her to return to Nine Mile, where her reception from Omeriah, although far from warm, was nowhere near as bad as she'd been dreading.

The following day, the still-suspicious father called the captain and Cedella to a meeting in the family living room, which resulted in tacit approval for their unusual and—by the standards of Jamaica in the mid-1940s—scandalous relationship.

For a while, Cedella and Norval were happy enough.

Then Cedella became even more heavily involved with the Shiloh Apostolic Church, where she was still a member of the choir, and her new-found religious convictions led to a major rift in the relationship. She told the seething captain that their sexual liaisons would have to stop, and he did everything he could to persuade her to change her mind. His frustration mounted to the point where he even resorted to lashing Cedella with the whip he used to control his horse—apparently with the approval of his friend Omeriah, himself a firm believer that women were not entitled to withhold sexual favors. "Your father say to give you a good horsing," he told the crying girl. But Cedella wouldn't yield, and the next time the captain attempted to rough her up she retaliated, sending him sprawling with a couple of blows to the chest. Eventually, after realizing Cedella was determined in her new beliefs, Marley left her alone for a long time. But the cunning and still-lecherous captain had new tricks up his sleeve, one of which was to tell Cedella he was sick and was worried that he might have to undergo a hernia operation—a procedure that, given his age and Jamaica's medical facilities in those days, could be highly dangerous.

Taking pity, she agreed to visit him.

That night, in April 1944, Bob Marley was conceived.

The following month Cedella realized she was pregnant—and the captain promptly announced that because of his hernia problems he could no longer carry out his overseeing duties on horseback and would have to move to Kingston to take a new job.

But first, he told Cedella, he wanted to get married.

"Married? To who?" she responded.

His reply was succinct: "To you."

Cedella immediately protested that she was too young to marry, but the captain once again persuaded her she should do what he wanted her to, and he quickly approached Omeriah and got his approval—reluctant, by all accounts—for the wedding. The eighteen-year-old Cedella Malcolm and the fifty-something Captain Norval Marley were married on the veranda of Yaya's house, on Friday, 9 June 1944. She wore white, he wore a tweed suit, and the following day he left for Kingston.

Cedella was to see her husband only twice during her pregnancy, but he had left Omeriah with enough money to build a little wooden house for the mother-to-be, and Cedella moved into the home, which now stands next to her son's mausoleum, to await the infant's arrival. She was at church when the first signs of labor appeared, and it continued for almost two days before, as she puts it, she gave birth to "a beautiful baby boy with a straight nose."

Cedella's overjoyed family could barely wait to hug and hold their new relative—and nor could Norval Marley, who showed up a few days later and, somewhat peremptorily, told Cedella the name he'd chosen for their son: Nesta Robert Marley. The Robert was after Norval's brother. To this day, no one's ever deduced where the Nesta came from, and when Cedella first heard the name she was far from enchanted.

The captain, as usual, had his way, telling her simply that it was a name he liked.

Omeriah and the rest of Cedella's family were ecstatic over the beautiful new brown-skinned member of the black Malcolm clan.

Norval Marley's family members were less than ecstatic over the beautiful new brown-skinned member of the white Marley clan, and his mother promptly disinherited him, leaving everything she had to the two sons of Robert, Norval's only brother. After spending a week or so in Nine Mile, Norval Marley returned to Kingston, leaving Cedella to look after their baby. His subsequent visits to his wife and son were few, far between, and brief, and to all intents and purposes Cedella was a single mother. Fortunately, she had a strong and loving network of family and friends to help her—and helping raise a young Bob Marley was a rewarding experience. He was a bright, happy little boy, loving and loved.

Like his mother, he attended Stepney school—but unlike her, he had a happy and productive time there, and was so intelligent he was soon helping the other children with their writing and arithmetic. Like his mother, he helped on the farm. The young Nesta would wake with the rising sun on misty St. Ann mornings, and tackle his first task of the day: milking the goats and cows. He would also help with the domestic chores, and, Cedella says, from an early age he could handle any meal from breakfast to dinner. Fish tea—a spicy, nourishing broth that was to be a lifelong favorite—was one of his specialities.

The young Nesta had a typical Jamaican rural childhood. He and his young friends played time-honored games with homemade bats, balls, kites, and slingshots—no computers, no video games, no cell phones, no iPods, no television sets—and formed friendships that would often last for the rest of their lives.

Life in rural Jamaica in those days was happy in a way that's becoming increasingly rare as much of the Caribbean, and the rest of the world, succumbs to TV culture. But it was also hard. And it was particularly hard for a single mother. Cedella opened a shop in Stepney, and while the business itself was far from a roaring success —just about everything she sold was on credit, and getting country people to pay what they owed was no easier than prying money from city slickers in Kingston—she was intrigued to see her five-year-old son reading the palms of customers. At first, she thought it was just child's play—until the customers started letting her know that everything Nesta was telling them about themselves was true.

She was astonished. It was the first indication there was something unusual—something almost mystic—about her son.

Even if making a half-decent living was tough for a young mother, these were happy times for Cedella and her young Nesta. But they weren't to last. When Nesta was six, Norval Marley, his absentee father, reappeared on the scene. During one of his rare visits to Nine Mile, Marley told his young wife he'd made arrangements for their son to go to boarding school in Kingston. Nesta's teachers tried to persuade Cedella that she shouldn't let him leave, that he would get a better education in Stepney than in the capital.

But, once again, Norval Marley had his way—and at the age of six Nesta Robert Marley found himself in the city that would eventually become his home and with which he'd forever be identified: Kingston.

2.
Lost and Found: Bob Goes to Kingston

Kingston, the capital of Jamaica, is one of the Caribbean's most fascinating cities. It's got history to spare, character in abundance, a wealth of exceptional West Indian architecture, culture to rass and, not coincidentally, it's the birthplace of reggae music.

It's also, in some areas and some ways, a tropical hell hole, with ghettos that can rival—in their squalor, their decadence, their hopelessness—the worst in the world. Just surviving—finding some way to put a little food in your belly, a shirt on your back, shoes on your feet, and a roof over your head—is an achievement, even if you're fully grown and the city's been home for all your life.

Imagine, then, what it would be like for a six-year-old from "country," a child from a tiny community of a few hundred souls, most of them family or friends, finding himself virtually abandoned in such a harsh and unwelcoming urban environment.

That's what happened to the young Nesta Robert Marley.

It was an experience that could have traumatized him. Instead, it toughened him and taught him, and ultimately helped prepare him to deal with the problems and pitfalls he would encounter on his way to becoming the Third World's first superstar.

Nesta's introduction to Kingston came courtesy of his father. Captain Norval Marley had already made one unsuccessful attempt to persuade Nesta's mother, Cedella, to let him take their young son to Kingston, telling her his well-to-do brother, Robert, wanted to adopt him. Cedella couldn't understand why a family that had disinherited the captain because he had married a black woman would suddenly want to adopt the son of that union.

She told him, in no uncertain terms, that Nesta was staying with her in Nine Mile. For once, the captain didn't get his own way.

But, as usual, he was persistent, and, when Nesta had just turned six, he made another of his rare visits to Nine Mile, this time telling Cedella he'd arranged for the boy to go to boarding school in Kingston, and that he and his family would take care of all the expenses. This time, Cedella was tempted. And so was her father, Omeriah, whose opinions carried considerable weight with everyone in Nine Mile, and particularly with his immediate family.

He agreed with his old friend the captain that Nesta would probably get a better education in Kingston. Teacher Isaacs at the Stepney school, confronted with the prospect of losing her star pupil, was vehemently against the idea. Nesta would get better teaching in the country than in the dog-eat-dog capital, she protested, and begged Cedella not to send him away.

This time, once again, the captain had his way.

Cedella packed her beloved young son's bags, Norval Marley came from Kingston to get him, and the pair set off for the teeming capital.

Not much is known about young Nesta's first trip to Kingston, or his arrival there, although one of the most popular biographies of Bob Marley, written not long after his death in 1981, purports to describe the journey in minute detail, with vivid descriptions of the coarse language and hair-raising driving of the country bus driver, and of the raucous behavior of the youngster's fellow passengers.

In that account, Nesta was traveling without either of his parents, with only an elderly cousin of Cedella's, a higgler on her way to Kingston to sell her okra, thyme, and peppers in one of the city's thronging markets, to keep an eye on the nervous youngster and make sure he arrived in the city safe and sound.

The description of that journey is so detailed and so vivid that anyone reading it couldn't help but be impressed by what must have been a remarkable piece of reporting, and couldn't help assuming that the biographer must have tracked down and interviewed some of the people who were on the bus that day and himself retraced the ramshackle vehicle's tortured route to Kingston and its arrival in the capital.

Only thing is, the supposedly factual account of that journey parallels, in almost every significant way—the foul-mouthed, reckless driver, the rancorous and often hilarious exchanges among the passengers, the filth and the squalor they encounter as they enter Kingston—the fictional trip made by Ivan O. Martin in Michael Thelwell's wonderful 1980 novel *The Harder They Come*, which was based on the seminal 1972 movie of the same name that introduced millions of people around the world to reggae music and to the harsh realities of the country that gave birth to it.

Anyone who's read *The Harder They Come* as well as the Marley biography, written by an American author a few years later, can't help wondering how much the graphic account of young Nesta's 1951 bus trip owes to the writing of Michael Thelwell, a Jamaican who knew exactly what he was talking about.

All that's known for certain about Nesta's first journey to Kingston is that it ended with his father, for reasons that remain a mystery to this day, reneging on the promise to Cedella to look after him and send him to boarding school. Instead, Norval took him to the home of an ageing and ailing woman, known only as Miss Gray, and left him there.

To all intents and purposes, Nesta Robert Marley, aged six, was a little boy lost in one of the toughest cities in the world—a city made all the more forbidding because, when he arrived, it was still recovering from one of the deadliest hurricanes to hit the Caribbean in decades.

In Rhoden Hall, Cedella was left to wonder what had become of her son. For weeks, and then months, she didn't hear a word from either her husband or Nesta. She wrote regularly, but there was no reply until, beside herself with worry, she sent a letter to the captain telling him she was coming to Kingston to see their son. This threat resulted in a prompt reply from Norval. She needn't bother making the trip, he told her, because Nesta wasn't in Kingston, he was in boarding school in a nearby parish, St.

Thomas, and doing very well. It was a blatant lie, but Cedella had no way of knowing this, and even though she still missed Nesta she didn't worry quite as much about him.

More months slipped by, and soon almost a year had passed since Nesta had left Nine Mile, and still his mother hadn't heard as much as a word from him.

Soon, however, events were to take a dramatic and surprising turn.

A friend of Cedella's, a higgler called Maggie Smith, was going about her business just off the Spanish Town Road, a stretch of highway that links Kingston with Spanish Town, the capital of Jamaica in bygone days when Spain ruled the island. Suddenly, she heard a familiar child's voice calling her name: "Miss Maggie, Miss Maggie." She looked around and, smiling up at her, was a young boy she immediately recognized as the missing son of her friend Cedella. He was plumper than she remembered, to be sure, but there was no mistaking the good-looking little boy with the heart-melting smile.

Nesta told the delighted higgler that he was on his way to market to buy some charcoal for a Miss Gray, and begged her to tell his mother where he was and to come for him. The only thing was, Maggie told Cedella, she couldn't remember the address Nesta had given her. But she did recall one thing: he was living on a Heywood Street, and she was sure her cousin Merle, who had been with her when they'd met Nesta, would be able to remember exactly where on Heywood Street.

She was wrong. Merle too couldn't remember the exact addres —but she did write to Cedella telling her that Heywood Street wasn't very long, and she was sure they'd be able to track Nesta down. The excited Cedella was soon in Kingston, and she and Merle headed straight for Heywood Street and started to ask if anyone knew a young boy called Nesta and where they might find him.

Suddenly, the moment Cedella had been waiting for so anxiously was on her: she spotted Nesta among a bunch of young-sters playing on a street corner, and called out his name.

The reunion was excited and emotional, with mother and son

embracing, kissing, and telling each other laughingly how much weight they'd each gained in the year they'd been apart.

Nesta soon took Cedella to the tiny bungalow where he'd been living, and introduced her to Miss Gray. Cedella immediately saw that the elderly lady was very, very sick, and she felt awful as it dawned on her that, rather than Miss Gray looking after young Nesta, he'd been taking care of her.

Her abandoned and lost son had proved that his simple rural upbringing had equipped him with both survival skills and compassion, and Cedella couldn't help feeling a surge of motherly pride as she realized, once more, that she'd been blessed with an exceptional child.

The pathetic old lady tried to convince Cedella that she couldn't get by without Nesta. She was too frail even to buy food for herself, she said, and she assured Cedella that if Nesta could stay and look after her she'd leave the youngster what little she had in the world.

Cedella, though, was determined she wasn't going back to Nine Mile without her son, and told Miss Gray she was sorry, but she'd have to take Nesta with her.

The following day they arrived safely in Nine Mile, and the young Nesta quickly fell back into the country life he loved. He returned to the Stepney school, to the delight of the teachers and children; he helped out on Omeriah's farm; he once more joined in the simple games and rambunctious play of rural youngsters, picking up where he'd left off with his old friends and making new ones.

One of those new friendships was with a youngster a couple of years younger than himself, whose father had recently opened a shop in Nine Mile. The new playmate was called Neville O'Reilly Livingston, but everyone knew him as Bunny, and no one in Nine Mile, watching the boys in their childish pursuits, could have had the faintest idea that these two typical country youngsters would before very long become iconic figures in Caribbean and global culture.

The first hint that music might be in Nesta's future came one afternoon when he was helping his mother in her shop in Stepney.

One of Cedella's regular customers, a woman called Aunt Zen, had been enormously impressed with young Nesta's palm-reading gifts before his prolonged absence in Kingston, and seeing him back in the shop she immediately offered him her hand to read.

Recalls Cedella in her autobiography, *Bob Marley, My Son,* "She came in the shop and they always play with him yunno, love him up and things like that, and she said, 'You going to read my hand for me today?' He said, 'No, I'm not reading no more hand,' and he just came from Kingston, and he had this likkle song, and he have two likkle sticks, and then he start to knock them and sing, 'Please, mister, don't you touch me tomato, touch me yam, me pumpkin, potato . . . all you do is feel up, feel up.' And then they just dead with laughing, it make them feel so good, and she gave him some money, I don't know what it was, a threepence or something. That was the first time he talk about music."

3.
Trench Town and Ska

For the young Nesta Robert Marley the early 1950s were comparatively uneventful. He was back in Rhoden Hall after his traumatic year virtually lost in Kingston, and living happily with his mother, Cedella, who was still running her small shop in Stepney. The years slipped by, with Cedella scraping a meager living for herself and young son from her tiny business. Captain Norval Marley had, in effect, disappeared from their lives. He made no attempt to support his wife and son, or to try to contact them in any way. In 1955, Cedella read in the obituary notices of the *Gleaner* newspaper that her absentee husband had died—she thinks from either cancer or malaria. At the age of ten Nesta had lost the father he never really knew.

He was soon to lose his mother, too—at least temporarily.

Cedella's brother John, who was living in Kingston, told her that his wife, Alberta, was going to England to become a nurse, and asked her if she'd like to join him in the capital and help look after his house. It was an offer she couldn't refuse. Country living was just too hard, and Cedella was a vibrant young woman who felt life had more to offer than the rural delights of Rhoden Hall, particularly when she was barely getting by financially. She made the move to Kingston, leaving young Nesta in the care of her father, Omeriah—who was delighted to have his grandson living with him and helping tend his farm.

For Nesta, although he missed his mother, the next couple of years passed by happily enough. For Cedella, things weren't quite so idyllic. Like tens of thousands who'd made the trek from "country" to Kingston before her, she quickly realized that life in that sweltering, crowded, chaotic city wasn't going to be easy. She toiled in a succession of domestic jobs with long hours and miserable pay, spending her time ironing, cooking, cleaning, and washing, and looking forward to the day when she'd be able to bring her beloved son to join her in the city.

Eventually, in 1957, that day arrived.

Cedella's Aunt Ivy, who lived in Kingston, invited her niece to share the spacious apartment she was renting on Beckford Street. She had room to spare, she told Cedella, but she needed help with the rent.

Cedella jumped at the chance—not only was there room for her, but also for young Nesta, and she immediately wrote to Omeriah in Nine Mile, asking him to send the boy to Kingston. The Malcolm family patriarch was understandably reluctant. Nesta was his favorite grandson—and a valuable helper on the land.

But Cedella was determined to be reunited with her son, and two weeks later, dressed in his best clothes and laden down with the inevitable produce that accompanies country Jamaicans coming to town, he arrived at the bustling Parade bus terminal for another joyous reunion with his mother.

This time he was in Kingston to stay.

But life was still tough in Jamaica for the vast majority of people, whether they were living in the lush countryside or the crowded capital. Cedella continued to work at every house-cleaning job she could find and, with two mouths to feed and young Nesta now enrolled in the Ebenezer government school, survival in Kingston was every bit as hard as it had been in Nine Mile. To make matters worse, Cedella quarreled with her Aunt Ivy and had to move out of the Beckford Street apartment. For the next couple of years she and Nesta were virtual nomads, moving from rented room to rented room.

Along the way, Cedella became the mistress—one of four, by all accounts—of Thaddeus "Taddy" Livingston, Bunny's father, who had sold his shop in Nine Mile and returned to the capital with young Bunny. Their relationship was a tempestuous and often violent one. Taddy, according to Cedella, was wildly jealous, despite his own blatant philandering, and had, as she puts it, "a wicked temper."

Cedella desperately needed a break—and she got one when another of her brothers, Solomon, who was splitting up with his wife, Ruth, told her they were moving out of their prized apartment in a government house in Trench Town. It was nearly new, having been built after the disastrous hurricane of 1951, and compared to the places where she and Nesta had been living it was almost luxurious, even though it was in the heart of a notorious ghetto. The government houses in Trench Town were two-story, concrete structures, cleverly designed so that each cluster of homes had its own communal yard. The apartments in these government houses were in considerable demand and Solomon told his sister she should move in just before he left—otherwise someone else would be sure to lay claim to the vacant premises.

Cedella and Nesta were soon installed at 19 Second Street. In a sense, although his roots would always be in Nine Mile, Bob Marley was home.

The year was 1959, and while Trench Town was a rough place by any standards, it was also home to some of Jamaica's most gifted musicians and to many of Kingston's Rastafarian community — members of a religious movement that in those days was looked upon with suspicion, fear, and scorn by the majority of Jamaicans. The Rastafarian movement had emerged in Jamaica in the early 1930s, following the coronation of Emperor Haile Selassie I in Ethiopia. Selassie, the only African monarch of a fully independent state, took the title King of Kings, Lord of Lords, Conquering Lion of the Tribe of Judah. Basing their beliefs on passages in the Bible's Book of Revelations, the Rastas worshipped him as a living god. The name of the religion comes from Selassie's pre-coronation name of Ras Tafari Makonnen, and he's commonly referred to by believers as Jah, a shortened form of Jehovah.

The religion is, essentially, non-violent and non-racist. Sadly, substantial numbers of violent and/or racist people in Jamaica and elsewhere have adopted the highly identifiable "dreadlock" hairstyle of Rastafarians, with unfortunate repercussions for the vast majority of honest, law-abiding Rastas. As recently as the 1970s in Canada, for example, a police "ten most wanted" list included a picture of a dreadlocked man, who was described as "a Rastafarian." It's not hard to imagine the outcry if the religious backgrounds of the other nine most wanted criminals—Roman Catholic, Protestant, Presbyterian, Jewish, Jehovah's Witness, or whatever they happened to be—had been spelled out.

Rastas believe in a healthy, clean-living lifestyle. While many eat fish, almost all Rastafarians shun meat (especially pork) and any processed or canned foods, preferring to eat "ital": fresh vegetables—cooked without salt—rice, legumes, etc. The majority of Rastas don't drink alcohol and believe strongly in the use of marijuana both as a religious sacrament and for its alleged health-associated benefits.

For the teenage Nesta Marley, the Rastafarians, and particularly Rasta musicians, were just one of the fascinations of Trench Town, and his bags were barely unpacked in the Second Street home before he set out on a voyage of personal and musical discovery that would carry him to pinnacles of international acclaim and recognition no musician—not the Beatles, not Mozart, not Pavarotti, not Presley, not Dylan, not Tchaikovsky, not the Stones, not Ella, not Sinatra—had come close to achieving.

Trench Town was also to provide him with the heaviest street creds of any pop star in history, as well as a rock-solid moral base for songs that would speak to the world's downtrodden and disenfranchised. From the favelas of Rio to the shantytowns of Lagos, from the slums of Calcutta to the bleak townships of South Africa, Bob Marley could talk to the global "sufferahs," even after he became rich and famous, because he came from Trench Town and he was one of them. He knew what it was like to be homeless and hungry. He knew how it felt to have rockstone for a pillow, cold ground for a bed.

At first, Trench Town wasn't always a welcoming place for a brown-skinned youngster from "country." Nesta, with his fair complexion and aquiline features, was different, and he often felt alienated and alone. Why, many of those around him wondered, was he living among them in the ghetto, and not "uptown" with most of the rest of the people who looked like him? Rita Marley, Bob's widow, recalls: "Sometimes he'd come across the resistance of being half-caste. There was a problem with his counterparts. Having come through this white father caused such difficulties that he'd want to kill himself and be thinking: Why am I this person? Why is my father white and not black like everybody else's? What did I do wrong? I can recall Bob asking me to use shoe polish in his hair, to make it more African, more black.

"Bob had to put up with a lot of resistance. If he wasn't that strong in himself he wouldn't be what he became. He would be downtrodden and seen as another half-caste who would never make it."

There was one particularly hurtful incident. Nesta, by now showing a keen interest in girls, fell for an attractive fourteen-year-old neighbor named Esther. "They were in love," Bob's mother recalls. But Esther's older brother detested Nesta because of his mixed race, and the teenage romance ended when he announced, "We don't want no white man in our blood."

The pressure could have been too much for Nesta, and sometimes it almost was. But it also toughened him, mentally and physically. The wiry youngster, fit and strong from a life of farming and blessed with speed and agility honed by countless hours playing soccer, soon acquired a reputation in the ghetto as someone not to be trifled with—a reputation that earned him the nickname that was to stick with him for life: "Tuff Gong."

Like most youngsters in Jamaica in those days—and like many still—Nesta left school when he was fifteen. In Kingston his interest in school had been nowhere near as keen as when he was Teacher Isaacs's star pupil at Stepney, and his formal education was cut short when the school he was attending closed abruptly.

By then, with Cedella and Thaddeus Livingston still in their volatile relationship, Nesta and Bunny had picked up their friendship from their Nine Mile days and were starting to take a serious interest in music. They were practicing regularly, even playing occasionally in local bars, but times in Trench Town were still tough, and the hard-pressed Cedella decided that Nesta would have to get a job. Before long he had an apprenticeship at a welding shop on South Camp Road and, between his day job, his music, helping his mother run a small restaurant she had bought, playing his beloved soccer, and continuing to immerse himself in the "running" of Trench Town, Nesta's life was a busy one.

While all of this was going on, the music scene in Jamaica was changing, and changing dramatically.

For years, music from America had been dominant in Jamaica. In the 1940s, big bands ruled the island, and bandleaders like Eric Dean and Val Bennett provided a training ground and a living—meager though it may have been—for people like guitarist Ernest Ranglin, trombonist Don Drummond, saxophonists Tommy McCook and Roland Alphonso, and dozens of other up-and-coming young musicians. For years, Jamaicans had happily danced the night away to the tunes of Duke Ellington, Count Basie, Glenn Miller, and Tommy Dorsey, but as the fifties approached, big bands were on the way out, and their smooth sounds were being replaced by the raunchier, heavier rhythms now coming out of the States, with New Orleans stars like Louis Jordan among the new favorites.

In 1950, Jamaica gave birth to a phenomenon that eventually would change not only its own music, but also have a lasting impact—to this day—on popular music around the world: the sound system.

Consisting essentially of banks of huge speakers, a powerful amplifier, and a turntable, the sound system delivered exactly what Jamaicans wanted: the latest, hottest records from the United States, played at pain-threshold volume in venues where they could dance, socialize, sink a Red Stripe or a Guinness, light up a big spliff, and fire back a shot or two of lethal Wray and Nephew overproof white rum—the words "guaranteed full strength," the only guide on the label to its brain-numbing potency, being a massive understatement.

The first sound-system operator of any significance was Tom "The Great" Sebastian, and many veterans of those early days still insist he's never been surpassed. He always had the latest "scorchers," hot off the plane from Miami, his speakers were the most powerful, and his DJs were the most original and masters of getting a crowd fired up.

Tom "The Great" Sebastian had only one thing going against him—he was essentially a peaceful man—and when a gun-toting former policeman, Duke "The Trojan" Reid, appeared on the sound-system scene, intimidating rivals with gangs of thugs, Sebastian diplomatically changed venues, moving from Pink Lane in one of Kingston's toughest areas to a more upscale and peaceful location. He soon discovered that his aggressive rival had done him a favor: he made a lot more money.

Duke Reid was the new don of the sound-system business, but before long he found himself in competition with an upstart rival —this time one he couldn't intimidate. Clement "Sir Coxson" Dodd took his nickname from a famous Yorkshire cricketer he admired. Alec Coxon, a fast bowler who played once for England, was famous as much for his prickly temper and caustic tongue as he was for his considerable ability on the field, and it's not known whether Dodd admired him for his cricketing prowess or his legendary no-nonsense persona. (Coxon died in his sleep in 2006, three days after his ninetieth birthday and only a few hours after knocking back his final three or four pints of beer at Westoe Rugby Club in South Shields, in the northeast of England. Three years earlier, at the age of eighty-seven, he had attempted to throttle an official of a rival club who made the mistake of calling him a "stupid old bugger.")

Like his cricket hero, Coxson Dodd was a hard man and nobody's fool, and he was soon to become much, much more to Jamaican music than a mere czar of the sound-system scene. After a few years of playing mainly American music on his Down Beat sound system, Coxson decided it was time Jamaicans had a sound of their own, something that was unique to them, which at the same time would keep them coming through his turnstiles.*

---

* *The three different spellings of "Coxon," "Coxson," and "Coxsone" are correct. The Yorkshire cricketer from whom Clement Dodd took his nickname was Alec Coxon. Dodd's version of the name when he used it personally was "Coxson" or "Sir Coxson." His record label was "Coxsone Records."*

Late in 1959, the year Cedella and Nesta moved to Trench Town, he asked two of Jamaica's most renowned musicians, master guitarist Ernest Ranglin and bassist Cluett "Clue J" Johnson, to come to a meeting at the liquor store he was then running. He told the two hugely gifted guitarists he wanted them to create a new, authentically Jamaican, sound. He wanted them to come up with something that was different from the island's traditional mento, different from the long-entrenched American music that was by now being diluted by a wave of antiseptic white soft-rockers with names like Bobby and Ricky, different from the calypso that had been made popular in Jamaica by brilliant Trinidadian artists like Lord Kitchener and Lord Beginner. They quickly got to work, and the result was ska, the precursor of rock steady, which in turn was to become reggae.

Ska, with its then unusual emphasis on what had always been regarded as the offbeat, had an instantly catchy and recognizable, almost galloping, rhythm, and Coxson, with both his key antennae —music and business—sending him loud and clear messages, had soon arranged session time at Jamaica's first recording facility, Federal Studio.

There, using primitive one-track equipment, a tune called "Easy Snappin'" by singer-pianist Theophilus Beckford was recorded by Beckford and a line-up of ace musicians that included two of the greatest horn men in Jamaican music history, Roland Alphonso and Rico Rodriguez.

It was the first ska record, and it was an instant hit.

Just as a young Nesta Robert Marley and an even younger Neville O'Reilly Livingston were starting to take a serious interest in making music, a new era was conceived and born. Within months a flood of ska recordings were being snapped up by a public eager for this upstart—this Jamaican—sound.

Nesta and Bunny, meanwhile, were on a learning curve. Not only were they listening to and absorbing the exciting ska rhythms, they were continuing to be influenced by American groups and solo singers like the Impressions, Brook Benton, the Drifters, James Brown, Sam Cooke, the Platters, and a young Elvis Presley.

Shades of the late sixties: Bob, in high spirits, sporting an Afro and fashionable bell-bottoms. Among the pictures behind him are Marcus Garvey and Haile Selassie, along with a poster advertising a Kingston dancehall appearance by U Roy, the legendary DJ.

Before long it dawned on the ambitious youngsters, by now firmly set on making music their careers, that they'd need professional help and training if they wanted to make serious progress. Fortunately for them—and the world—there was a music university in their ghetto and it was just around the corner, on Third Street.

Its professor was one of Jamaica's music pioneers, the now legendary Joe Higgs. Already a star in Jamaica by virtue of a string of pre-ska hit records as one half of the duo of Higgs and Wilson, Higgs was a serious professional who was more than willing to share his expertise with up-and-coming youngsters in Trench Town. Higgs's yard wasn't your typical university. Lectures were conducted amid clouds of ganja smoke and the sound of clinking bottles of Red Stripe beer, but no Harvard or Oxford professor could have been more serious about passing on knowledge than Higgs, a master of harmony singing and vocal pitch.

Higgs was a stern and unrelenting taskmaster (as Bob Marley himself would be in the not-too-distant future), and his Third Street yard was a magnet for aspiring Trench Town musicians. Among them was a tall youngster, six months older than Nesta, who had an attitude and, more important, a guitar.

His name was Winston Hubert McIntosh, also known as Peter, and soon to be changed and shortened to simply Peter Tosh.

Peter first met Nesta and Bunny when he heard them singing with Higgs in the Third Street yard and joined in the practice session. Soon the three youngsters were harmonizing together, and it was quickly obvious that the combination of their very different voices—Nesta's hard-edged, distinctive tenor, Bunny's sweet harmony falsetto (as it was in those days), and Peter's authoritative baritone—was something very, very special. Years later Peter Tosh recalled: "There was a time when we were what you would call imperfect in the music, learning the music that come through divine inspiration, and we find out that me and Bunny together had the kind of voice that could decorate Bob's voice and make it beautiful. So we just did that wholeheartedly."

While the three worked on their pitch and their harmonies with Higgs, Peter—an accomplished guitarist who was soon in demand for session work—taught Nesta the instrument. Years later he would complain bitterly that he was never given credit for this.

Before long the three had become fast friends, and along with another strong singer, Junior Braithwaite, and two backup singers, Beverley Kelso and Cherry Smith, they were performing as a group called the Teenagers.

But—perhaps prophetically—the young Nesta also had solo aspirations.

At the welding yard on South Camp Road he had befriended another ambitious young singer, Desmond Dekker, who had already recorded a hit song for Beverley's, a successful ska label owned by a young Chinese–Jamaican entrepreneur, Leslie Kong. Dekker took Nesta for an informal audition with Kong. It wasn't the first time the youngster had tried to get the producer's attention, but last time round he hadn't been taken seriously and had been somewhat ignominiously told to "leave the premises" by one of Kong's employees. With the solidly established Dekker in his corner, things were different. Kong was willing to listen—and the shrewd businessman liked what he heard, particularly a number Marley had written called "Judge Not."

Kong quickly arranged session time at Federal Studio, and, in February 1962, Nesta Robert Marley made his first recordings. He had just turned seventeen. Singing in a high-pitched and unmistakably teenage voice, almost aching with intensity, Nesta was backed by some of the cream of Jamaican session players—Arkland "Drumbago" Parks on drums, Lloyd Brevett on bass, Jerome "Jah Jerry" Haines on guitar, Roland Alphonso on tenor sax, and Charlie Organaire on harmonica.

"Judge Not" was both an acknowledgment of Marley's deep country roots—opening with a lilting, mento-style penny whistle that underpinned the tune from beginning to end—and a pointer to the sort of righteous lyrics that he was to embellish upon and refine over the next eighteen years. The overall tempo was classic, driving ska, as the first song ever recorded by Bob Marley admonished listeners not to be critical of others lest they be put under scrutiny themselves and found wanting: "Judge not, before you judge yourself."

A month or two later, Kong brought Nesta back to Federal studio, this time to record songs called "One Cup of Coffee" and "Terror," using the same backing musicians, with the notable show

Stirring it up sixties style: a young Bob Marley on a crowded stage at a Kingston

addition of the legendary Don Drummond on trombone. In an attempt to sell more records by giving the artist a slicker-sounding name, "One Cup of Coffee" was credited to a "Bobby Martell."

It would be nice to be able to write that Bob Marley's first recording sessions produced a hit. They didn't: sales were modest, at best. But these sessions still constituted a major step forward in his career—and they were also notable for the quality of the musicians who backed the youngster as he sang his heart out in that fervent, penetrating, and sometimes shaky young tenor. From his first recording sessions to his last live concert, almost two decades later, Marley would always be able to attract the finest musicians to accompany him—and to get the very best out of them.

Nesta's music career might have been on the move, but things were still tough at home—and they were about to get a whole lot tougher. Cedella had become pregnant by Thaddeus Livingston and had given birth to a daughter, Pearl. The new arrival served to cement Nesta's already close ties with Bunny—the infant was a half-sister to each of them. But Cedella remained unhappy in her volatile association with Thaddeus, and when her sister Ivy, who was by now living in Wilmington, Delaware, invited her to join her in the United States, she jumped at the opportunity for a new life and an escape from a violent relationship.

She told the disgruntled Thaddeus she'd be going to Wilmington for a short visit, and that her sister Enid would take care of Pearl while she was away. In 1962 an excited Cedella Marley, who had never set foot outside Jamaica in her life, caught a plane for the United States. Thaddeus wouldn't have been amused if he'd known that the "short visit" would extend well into the next millennium.

Once again Nesta Robert Marley was motherless.

Even worse, soon after Cedella's departure, the unpredictable Thaddeus, accompanied by another of his mistresses and her brother, moved in with him on Second Street. It was a situation that couldn't last, and it didn't. With his mother gone and life at home intolerable, Nesta moved out. At eighteen, having quit his job at the welding shop after an agonizing accident that almost cost him an eye, he was broke and homeless in one of the world's toughest ghettos. His future, by any rational yardstick, looked bleak.

But the intrepid and street-smart teenager knew how to get by in Trench Town; years later when he was rich and famous he attributed his resilience at that time to his country upbringing: "Things was kind of lean . . . To me it was lean but me coulda stand it because coming from country, where you learn things like you don't learn to depend on family and all of that, yunno, you go out and you plant your own corn, and you watch the corn grow and you pick your own corn, yunno. All a dem fruit pon dem tree, you can get them. The city's a whole different ball game. People have to go to work, catch the bus. In country, you go for the donkey, and ride the donkey to the farm and cool, yunno, where city people must catch the bus, go to work, get off at work, come back home. It's a different thing 'appen."

Despite his desperate circumstances Nesta was determined to press on with his career in music, and confident that if he did a break would come his way.

He was right.

4.
Fame . . . but Not Fortune

Life in Trench Town has never been easy—even when you've got a place, however humble, to call home. When you're homeless and broke, with no family to fall back on, it's as tough as it gets.

That was the situation Nesta Robert Marley, a skinny teenager, found himself in when his mother left for a "short trip" to visit her sister in the United States in 1962 and never returned. He could probably have scraped together enough money to take the country bus back to Nine Mile, where he'd have been certain of a joyous welcome from his grandfather, Omeriah, and the rest of the Malcolm clan and where he could count on finding work on the family farm. Instead, he chose to get by as best he could in Trench Town.

Nesta became a ghetto nomad, a penniless, down-on-his-luck street dweller.

In the classic Jamaican movie *The Harder They Come*, there's a harrowing scene in which the destitute Ivan O. Martin roams the streets of Kingston looking for a place to rest his head and any scraps of food he can find. That's exactly what was happening to Nesta in real life a decade before the movie came out and, like Ivan O. Martin, he sought solace and an escape through music. He was in a desperate situation—and music seemed like the only conceivable way out of it. The practice sessions, mainly with Peter and Bunny, continued, the harsh circumstances adding an element of urgency to their by now angelic harmonizing.

Early in 1963, a Trench Town friend, Vincent "Tata" Ford, took pity on the homeless youngster and invited him to share the kitchen he lived in on First Street. It was hardly luxurious—Nesta's bed also served as a gambling table, and he'd have to wait until the games of chance presided over by Tata were over before he could catch a few hours' sleep.

Often, while Nesta and his Trench Town bredren were singing in Tata's yard, an older friend, George Robinson, would build a roaring fire and keep it lit while the youngsters worked on their music, boiling up a pot of cornmeal porridge whenever his companions became too hungry to continue practicing. It was a scene that would be immortalized just over a decade later in the reggae anthem "No Woman No Cry," Bob Marley's first chart hit outside Jamaica and the song that propelled him, irrevocably, on the road from regional stardom to international superstardom.

Master classes in harmonizing were also continuing in Joe Higgs's Third Street yard, where Nesta, Bunny, Peter, Junior Braithwaite, and their two backup singers, Beverley Kelso and Cherry Green, waited eagerly for the break they felt must come their way. It took a long time in arriving, but eventually they got the chance they were longing for. And it was a big one.

Another Trench Town friend of Nesta's, Alvin Patterson, an accomplished percussionist and master of the Rastafarian burru style of drumming, was a professional musician and he knew Clement "Sir Coxson" Dodd, the sound-system king and pioneering record producer who had opened a studio of his own at 13 Brentford Road in 1963 and who held auditions every Sunday. It was called Studio One, and it was to become the most famous of Jamaica's many legendary recording facilities. Dodd was always on the lookout for new talent, and Patterson—now known to Wailers fans worldwide as Seeco, the group's percussionist—decided to take Nesta, Peter, Bunny, Junior, Beverley, and Cherry to audition for the reigning czar of the Jamaican music scene.

Although they were now almost veterans of live talent shows, where they'd appeared as the Teenagers and the Wailing Rudeboys, the six youngsters were nervous during the auditions, and by all accounts Dodd wasn't wildly impressed with the first four numbers he heard. Then Peter, always the most assertive member of the group, told Dodd they'd like to do one more song. It was one Nesta had written, a ska scorcher called "Simmer Down" that spoke directly to an emerging Jamaican phenomenon, the "rude boys," whose rebellious and frequently violent ways were becoming a major force in the island's ghetto culture.

Dodd liked the song, and a few days later, barely able to contain their excitement, the group—minus Cherry Green, who couldn't get time off work—returned to Studio One to record it. As usual, Coxson had gathered an ace group of musicians, by then known as the Skatalites, for what would be the most historic of the thousands of recording sessions that were to take place at Studio One.

The line-up for the landmark "Simmer Down" session, at which four other tracks—"I Don't Need Your Love," "I Am Going Home," "Do You Remember," and "Straight and Narrow"—were also recorded, was: Bob Marley, vocal; Junior Braithwaite, vocal and harmony vocal; Bunny Livingston, harmony vocal; Peter McIntosh, harmony vocal; Beverley Kelso, harmony vocal; Lloyd Nibbs, drums; Lloyd Brevett, bass; Jerome "Jah Jerry" Haines, guitar; Jackie Mittoo, piano; Don Drummond, trombone; Roland Alphonso, tenor sax; Tommy McCook, tenor sax; "Dizzy" Johnny Moore, trumpet; Dennis "Ska" Campbell, baritone sax.

From the opening notes, a couple of lightning whiplash whacks on the snare by Lloyd Nibbs accompanied, almost instantly, by full-tilt ensemble ska horns punctuated by Don Drummond's growling trombone, it was clear that "Simmer Down" was going to be a monster. It was. In fact, it was so hot, so obviously a winner, that Dodd had it pressed right away, and the ambitious youngsters were ecstatic when they heard it playing that same evening at Coxson's Down Beat sound system.

Recalls Bunny: "Everything started there. Everything. It's, you know, you just can't describe that moment, man, you just sang the song in the morning time and in the night you hear it blasting on the air. You can just imagine the kind of thrill."

Marley's intense lead vocal, an urgent plea to rebellious ghetto youth to "control your temper, or the battle will be hotter, and you won't get no supper, and you know you bound to suffer," had the sound-system posse expressing themselves on the dance floor in a flash—and it sounds as fresh and vibrant today as it must have all those years ago.

There has been considerable debate as to the actual date of the epoch-making "Simmer Down" recording session, but Bunny, who was there, is sure it took place in June or July 1964, and specifically recalls the backing musicians being the Skatalites, rather than a random group of session men. The Skatalites weren't formed officially until June 1964, and *Bob Marley and the Wailers: The Definitive Discography*, by the distinguished musicologists and reggae collectors Roger Steffens and Leroy Jodie Pierson, lists the session's date—with a question mark—as 6 July1964.

The original issue of "Simmer Down" was credited to the Wailers and, unlike young Nesta's solo recordings for Leslie Kong a couple of years earlier, there was no ambivalence in how it was received by the Jamaican public. Within weeks "Simmer Down" was No. 1 in the charts, and it stayed there for the next two months. Coxson's original pressing sold out, and the labels on the second pressing credited the song to "Bob and the Wailers."

Nesta Robert Marley had recorded his first hit. He was on top of the charts, he was on the radio, he was becoming a household name with Jamaica's record-buying public. And, having moved out of Tata's too-crowded First Street kitchen, all this was happening while he was broke, belly-growling hungry, and homeless.

He had fame. Fortune was still more than a decade away.

Coxson Dodd, meanwhile, knew he was on to a winner. The shrewd Dodd was a virtual one-man hit-making machine in Jamaica. His Studio One was in constant use for recording, routinely turning out hit after hit after hit. And that was just in one day's work—the studio was so busy it wasn't unusual for a session musician to play on 100 or more tracks in a week.

So much music with chart potential was bursting out of 13 Brentford Road in the 1960s that local radio DJs got fed up with the barrage of 45s coming their way on the all-too-familiar "Coxsone" and "Studio One" labels. The ingenious Dodd simply

Clement "Coxson" Dodd, the pioneering Jamaican producer and sound-system czar. The Wailers' earliest hits were recorded in his legendary Studio One.

invented a bunch of new labels: during the two years or so they were with him, the Wailers' work also appeared on the Muzik City, Supreme, Tabernacle, and Wincox labels—all, unbeknownst to the radio station DJs, part of the Coxson Dodd empire.

Dodd also played a key role in the early careers of a who's who of Jamaican music. Among the now legendary artists associated with Studio One over the years were Jackie Mittoo, Ernest Ranglin, Don Drummond, Joseph Hill, Roland Alphonso, Tommy McCook, Toots and the Maytals, Ernest Wilson, Marcia Griffiths, the Heptones, the Ethiopians, the Royals, Wailing Souls, Burning Spear, Slim Smith, Delroy Wilson, John Holt, Cornell Campbell, Alton Ellis, the Abyssinians, Winston Jarrett and the Righteous Flames, Augustus Pablo, Lee "Scratch" Perry, Sugar Minnott, Denis Alcapone, Willie Williams, Freddie McGregor, Ken Boothe, Horace Andy, Derrick Harriot, and Dennis Brown. Dodd's formula was a simple one: he had to like every single song that came out of Studio One, and what he liked most was music with a distinctive melody, a wicked bass, and the very finest of horns, usually courtesy of alumni of Kingston's fabled Alpha boys' school. And, of course, the vocals had to be up to those standards. He also liked making money, and it made no difference to him if a song was an original composition with the most conscious of lyrics, a catchy love song, or a "cover" of an international hit. If he thought it had a chance of making the charts, he'd record it and use his considerable influence to ensure it was played on the radio and at sound-system dances.

Over the next couple of years, he encouraged the Wailers to record a wildly eclectic range of material ranging from ska to doo wop to straightahead pop. The list of "cover" songs the group recorded in this era is intriguing. Among them were: Dion and the Belmonts' "Teenager in Love"; the Beatles' "And I Love Her" ("and I love her, yes siree," sang Bob, adding a novel lyrical twist to the Lennon and McCartney original); Lord Melody's ribald calypso classic "Shame and Scandal" (recorded in raunchy ska tempo at the same session as the first version of "One Love," which would eventually be chosen by the BBC as the song to define the twentieth century); Tom Jones's chestnut "What's New Pussycat;" Bob Dylan's "Like a Rolling Stone," and Bing Crosby's "White Christmas" ("I'm dreaming of a white Christmas, not like the ones I used to know," sang Bob in that wailing tenor). Mainly, though, the Wailers recorded rude-boy anthems and plaintive love songs.

Clement Dodd, as virtually every musician who worked for him will attest, was a frugal and tough man who hated parting with money every bit as much as he loved making it, and legend has it he kept a gun handy at Studio One as the ultimate arbiter in his constant feuds with his artists over royalties. But he did take pity on his homeless hit-maker, and soon after "Simmer Down" took the Jamaican charts by storm, Dodd told Nesta he could live in a room in the back of the Studio One complex. For much of 1964 and '65, that simple room was home for Nesta Robert Marley, in those days often known to his friends as "Robbie." It may not have been palatial, but it did have one massive attraction for a teenager determined to make a career in music: he was living in the midst of the most prolific music-making machine in the

Caribbean, surrounded by and learning from some of the most brilliant musicians in the world.

Before long, the young Nesta was playing a major role in the Studio One runnings, organizing recording sessions and working alongside people like Jackie Mittoo, the great keyboard player; Ernest Ranglin, Jamaica's supreme guitarist; and horn legends Tommy McCook, Roland Alphonso, Lester Sterling, and "Dizzy" Johnny Moore.

If Joe Higgs's Trench Town yard had been Nesta's first music university, Coxson Dodd's Studio One was his graduate school. As well as immersing himself in learning how a recording studio worked, he was getting a rudimentary apprenticeship from his new mentor in another critical aspect of his chosen profession. He was learning the music business—and he was learning the hard way from the notoriously tight-fisted producer. He was also about to fall in love.

Alfarita Anderson, known to everyone as Rita, was a Sunday school teacher and church choir singer with a "good girl" reputation. She lived with an aunt and uncle on Greenwich Park Road in an area known as Ghost Town, which the Wailers used to pass by regularly on their way from Trench Town to Studio One. A gifted singer herself, she was impressed by the impromptu harmony vocals she heard when they were passing, and recalls that they sounded "like angels." But they didn't look like angels. They looked and acted like rude boys—albeit rude boys with wonderful voices—and the cautious Rita Anderson kept her distance until, eventually, a friend took her to Studio One, where she was introduced to Nesta, Bunny, and Peter.

By then, Rita was part of a group of her own called the Soulettes, and Peter—the first Wailer to pay her any serious attention—arranged an audition for them with Coxson. Impressed, Dodd instructed Nesta, still living in the back room at 13 Brentford Road and playing an important role in the Studio One operation, to take them under his wing. He was to coach them and be their musical mentor. As always, the music came first with the young Marley, and he took his duties seriously. Almost too seriously. Rita recalls: "We were very scared of him because of the discipline he would put on his rehearsals, so he wasn't a favorite of ours at the time. We used to say that this man is very cross."

For months Nesta was cool and kept his distance.

So no one was more surprised than Rita when Bunny, acting as an intermediary, told her his best friend had fallen in love with her. She may have been shocked, but she was also pleased and flattered. It was the start of Nesta Robert Marley's first-known serious love affair, although it was to be far from the last.

Soon the two were almost inseparable. They made love for the first time in Marley's former digs, Tata's First Street kitchen—his old friend having discreetly disappeared for the evening—and their relationship, by now already close, was to become even closer as a result of a traumatic shared experience.

Nesta had confided in Rita that he thought he was being attacked at night by a "duppy." In a nation where obeah, or "science" as it's often known, is taken very seriously, a duppy is something you don't want to take an interest in you—a malevolent spirit, perhaps under the control of an obeah man, that can wreak havoc in the world of the living. This duppy, he said, was trying to pull him from his bed in Coxson's back room and was ruining his sleep, with the result he was suffering from headaches when he was awake and nightmares when he was sleeping.

Rita, a devout Christian in those days, could have told her lover he was imagining things. Instead, she said she'd stay with him that night in the back room at Studio One. Not long after the young couple had fallen asleep on Nesta's makeshift bed, Rita felt herself being wrenched awake and almost hurled onto the floor. She was terrified, unable to speak and virtually paralyzed. Eventually she regained her speech and woke the sleeping Nesta.

The traumatic experience convinced Rita that Nesta couldn't stay another night at Studio One, and she invited him to share her room in the Ghost Town house where she and her baby daughter from a brief liaison the previous year, Sharon, lived with her aunt and uncle.

The only problem was that Rita's Aunt Viola was particularly strict, so Marley had to be smuggled into Rita's room through a

Rita Marley in her "Soulettes" era

back window of the house. The first part of the plan went smoothly enough, but the evening turned into a disaster when Sharon started crying and Rita's nosy aunt burst into the room to see what was going on.

What was going on was glaringly obvious to anyone, especially an eagle-eyed Jamaican aunt of the old school, and the couple were told to get out of the house. The next day, after much begging and pleading by Rita, her aunt relented, realizing the young lovers were serious about each other and even going so far as to build a shed in her yard for Nesta to sleep in.

Nesta's domestic situation had improved, but at Studio One the Wailers were still having trouble getting paid a fraction of what they felt they were worth as Jamaica's biggest recording stars.

"Simmer Down," their first No. 1, had been followed by a slew of hits, and there wasn't the slightest doubt that Clement Dodd was making substantial amounts of money from their talent and hard work. He was the one reaping the financial rewards from the years they'd spent in Joe Higgs's and Tata's yards learning the intricacies of harmony and honing their individual and collective voices to near-angelic perfection.

But only a pittance was finding its way into their pockets— and they needed the money to survive. Years later Peter Tosh would bitterly recall the Wailers' Studio One era: "I've been through all kinds of humiliations. Talk about sing and get 20 dollars, I've been through more than that. I have tunes 1, 2 and 3, on the charts, Wailers in those times, and when we hold a position of 1, 2 and 3, and further down like 9 and 20, we would never leave the charts for months, and all those times we have been on the charts, sometimes my shoes only have uppers, no downers, my foot on the ground, and those are the kind of shit-stem I've been through."

Meanwhile, Nesta's mother, by now happily remarried in the United States, had been trying to persuade her beloved son to join her in Wilmington. Her new husband, Edward Booker, was willing to sponsor Cedella, her young daughter Pearl, and her son Nesta to come to the United States permanently, and Cedella had returned for a brief visit to Jamaica in order to re-enter the US as a landed immigrant with a treasured Green Card.

During that trip, she'd been unable to persuade Nesta to go to the States right away, but he had agreed to get a Jamaican passport as the first step in the arduous bureaucratic process towards obtaining a US entry visa. The clerk they'd dealt with at the government passport office in Kingston had snorted with derision when he'd seen the applicant's first name: Nesta.

"What kind of name is that?" he'd asked rudely, blithely unaware that the slender young man sitting quietly across his desk was someone most Trench Town rudies would be reluctant to provoke.

Cedella told the obnoxious bureaucrat that it was her son's "natural name, given him by his father" and asked, "What's wrong with it?"

"'Is a girl name, that's what wrong with it," the clerk replied, adding that the American authorities would just laugh when they saw it.

Cedella, well aware of the problems Jamaican bureaucrats are capable of causing, fought back the temptation to strangle the offensive clerk and instead meekly asked what they should do. The bureaucrat demanded to know if her son had a middle name. "Robert," she replied. "Bob, that's a good solid name for a man," the bureaucrat agreed, telling her he would enter the name on the passport as Robert Nesta Marley.

As they departed with the passport, neither realized that, in switching Nesta and Robert, a faceless clerk had helped create a name that would soon be known around the world.

Nesta Robert Marley walked into that government office in Kingston. Bob Marley walked out.

The passport opened up new options for Bob, but he decided things were going so well with his music in Jamaica—in every way but financially—that he'd be better off staying there and seeing how things worked out. And when he did occasionally get paid, he was generous with his earnings. Cedella recalls how he mailed a crisp new $10 bill to her in Wilmington, accompanied by a letter telling her that, while times were still hard, "a little money" had come his way and he wanted her to have some of it. It was an early indication of what would become Bob Marley's legendary generosity.

Mostly, although they were continuing to mash up the Jamaican charts with hit after hit after hit, what the Wailers were earning continued to be a "little money," and eventually Bob had

had enough. He decided the Wailers couldn't continue to make Coxson rich while they were getting coppers, and that the only solution was to make enough money for them to produce their own music.

And he figured the only place to make that sort of money would be the United States. It was time he joined his mother in Wilmington. He wrote and told Cedella he'd made the big decision, and she immediately sent him a plane ticket.

With the prompting of his frugal mentor Coxson Dodd, he also made another major decision: he proposed to Rita, and they were married on 10 February 1966. A few days later he caught a flight for the United States, leaving his new bride behind just as his father had left Cedella after their wedding in 1944.

On a February day in 1966 at Kingston's Norman Manley International Airport, Bob Marley said farewell to Rita and to the steamy tropical heat of Kingston. A few hours later his plane was touching down in Philadelphia, where a joyously warm welcome was in store for him. But while the welcome was warm, Bob was about to experience something new, something life in Nine Mile and Trench Town hadn't prepared him for, something he wasn't really ready for: cold.

5.

Coming in from the Cold

Before long, Bob Marley would be jetting around the world, almost as comfortable in the first-class cabin of a 747 as he was in a government yard in Trench Town. But in 1966, when he flew to Philadelphia to be met by his mother, who had found a new life for herself in the United States, it was the first time he'd been outside of Jamaica. And the first time he'd experienced a phenomenon that's a routine part of life for more than half the world's population: winter.

Bob landed in Philadelphia on a frigid February night. The bone-numbing weather had to be something of a shock to someone whose idea of cold was when it plummets into the high sixties in the mountains of Jamaica, but his welcome couldn't have been warmer. Accompanied by a small posse of friends and relatives, Cedella met her son in a scene reminiscent of their previous reunions in Kingston—with hugging and kissing that started the moment he walked out of the customs hall and continued into the parking lot and on the drive home. "There was so much merriment in the long drive back to Wilmington it was like we were all drunk," recalls Cedella.

The excitement continued long after they arrived at the house Cedella shared with her Mr. Booker, as she always called him. He was kind, loving, and generous, a major change from her relationship with Thaddeus Livingston and a huge improvement on Captain Norval Marley, and they were living contentedly.

Bob, who'd spent most of the previous two years roughing it either on the streets of Trench Town or in places like Tata's crowded and often raucous kitchen, Rita's aunt's tiny backyard shed, and Coxson's spartan and duppy-plagued back room, was overwhelmed.

Nothing he'd seen or heard about in Nine Mile or Kingston had prepared him for the sort of luxury the average middle-class American takes for granted, and he couldn't get over the size of his new home. He was impressed by the well-appointed bathrooms, and particularly pleased when he found out he would have a comfortable room of his own, an almost unheard of indulgence in the ghettos of Jamaica. "Boy, de house nice, eh," he told Cedella. Then he shared his big news with his mother, telling her that he'd married despite the fact he was going to America, and describing his new bride with pride. "If you meet the girl you'll like her," he assured his mother. "She come from a nice family."

Cedella was a little hurt that she hadn't been told of the marriage earlier, but she quickly relented—perhaps recalling some of the circumstances she'd found herself in as a teenager—and they were soon on their way downstairs to join the party by now in progress and celebrate both Bob's marriage and his arrival in America.

The partying didn't last long. Bob had only one reason for being in the United States: he was there to make as much money as he could as quickly as he could so he could return to Jamaica and Bunny and Peter and put them in control of their own musical destiny. He wanted to be able to return home with much-needed instruments and even more sorely needed cash, so the group could produce and market their own music and reap the rewards they felt they deserved for their huge popularity in Jamaica.

Bob Marley, a stranger in a strange land, a Jamaican whose deep patois was as incomprehensible to American ears as their speech patterns were alien to his, a youngster whose résumé consisted largely of farming, music, and welding, was in search of employment in the Land of Opportunity.

It was a serious job hunt, but it had its humorous moments. Cedella recalls how she phoned a Jamaican friend who worked as a stevedore on the Wilmington waterfront, asking if he thought he might be able to fix Bob up with a job. The stevedore told Cedella to send her son to the docks the next day, and he'd do his best to get him work.

The obvious problem was that a stevedore's job is physically demanding, and while Bob was muscular and fit from playing soccer morning, noon, or night, he didn't have the sort of physique you need to work on the docks. Cedella had a brainwave. To make him look bigger and stronger, she dressed her son in layer after layer of bulky clothing and a large pair of canvas boots. "He was padded up so thickly his arms stuck out like a robot. When he tried to walk he made a loud rustling noise. With nearly every step he wobbled," she recalls.

Fighting back her laughter, she told him he now looked the part of a stevedore, and Bob set off into the bitter cold and, he hoped, his first job in the United States.

It was a disaster.

When Bob left home, it was cold. As the day progressed, it got colder. And colder.

Bob was gone for hours, and Cedella was starting to worry as the day wore on and the weather turned uglier by the minute. Eventually, to her relief, there was a knock on the door. She opened it to see her son, his face alarmingly red and looking almost frost-bitten, on the doorstep.

He stumbled into the house, shivering uncontrollably, and told the by-now distraught Cedella that the boss at the docks had said he wasn't dressed for stevedores' work, and that even if he had been he wasn't big or strong enough for the heavy lifting that came with the job. Bob, who had been driven to the docks by Mr. Booker, had quickly concluded that, once more, his foot was his only carriage, and had set off to walk home in the appalling weather. He was used to walking, but not in minus-zero temperatures and driving snow. To make matters worse, he'd had a brush with a gang of thugs who were looking menacingly at him, and had run most of the way home, adding to the already vicious wind-chill factor.

Eventually Cedella managed to thaw Bob out beside the radiator, and was hugely relieved when it became clear he didn't have frostbite. Something else was clear: Bob Marley wasn't about to get a job working outdoors in the depths of a Delaware winter. Soon he found an indoor job, as a janitor at Wilmington's Dupont hotel (one biography of Marley says he worked under a false name as a laboratory assistant at the DuPont Chemical Factory, which, given his work experience and the hiring procedures of big American companies, seems unlikely).

When he wasn't at work, chances are Bob would be at home, saving his money, enjoying his time with Cedella, getting to know Mr. Booker, practicing his singing and his guitar and working on songs he was eager to record when he returned to Jamaica, hopefully with his pockets full of hard-earned American dollars that would allow him, Bunny, and Peter to escape the clutches of Coxson and take charge of their careers.

In Jamaica, meanwhile, Bunny and Peter weren't sitting around idly. The group's line-up had changed even before Bob left for Delaware, with the departure of Junior Braithwaite, who emigrated to Chicago with the rest of his family in the summer of 1965. Beverley Kelso and Cherry Green had also parted company with the group somewhere along the line between Junior's permanent departure and Bob's short-term absence, reducing the Wailers to the core trio of Bunny, Peter, and the temporarily missing Bob.

The absence of Junior and Bob, who had been considered the group's strongest vocalists, gave Bunny and Peter the long-awaited opportunity to showcase their own superb singing. They didn't hesitate.

Peter—recording as Peter Touch, as he was often known in those days—cut the first version of one of his signature tunes, "The Toughest," at Studio One in May 1966, and followed it up in August with "Treat Me Good," another track that showed Tosh at his most macho. "If you want to live, treat me good," Peter sang, sounding in dreadly earnest, in one of the earliest of the songs that were to help reinforce his reputation for having a short fuse and occasionally violent disposition.

Bunny, always regarded as the most spiritual of the Wailers, was espousing peace and love, along with doses of rude-boy militancy. His output as lead singer during Bob's absence included "Dancing Shoes," "I Stand Predominant," the gorgeous "Dreamland," a cover of Bob Dylan's "Like a Rolling Stone," "Sunday

Morning," "He Who Feels It Knows It" (also often known as "Who Feels It Knows It" or "Linger You Linger"), and "Let Him Go."

After nine months in Wilmington, when it dawned on him there was a possibility he might be drafted into the US army (a decidedly grim prospect in the early days of the Vietnam war) and with another brutal Delaware winter just around the corner, Bob Marley decided to return to Jamaica.

He flew back to Kingston in October 1966, and moved back in with Rita at Greenwich Park Road. The reunion was a happy one, and Bob's return also meant the core three Wailers were back in business.

Despite their disillusionment with Clement Dodd, the reunited group decided to give Coxson one last chance and, using some of the money Bob had saved in Wilmington, they made a deal with him to produce their own record at Studio One, with Dodd taking care of distribution.

It was the first release on the Wailers' own label, which they called Wail N Soul M. The A-side of the 45, which Bob had composed in Cedella's Wilmington home, was called "Bend Down Low," and it was yet another Wailers smash. But once again the Wailers didn't get paid—an even more infuriating situation because they'd financed the record themselves and it was on their own label.

This time they'd had enough. They never recorded for Coxson again and seldom had a good word to say about him. "Them rob we out of it again," Bob would declare later of the unpaid royalties for "Bend Down Low," "man, all is robbery."

He had a point. Years later, Chris Blackwell, to whom Coxson had licensed the English rights to dozens of Wailers songs, told the group he'd sent the producer hundreds of thousands of pounds in royalty payments. "We never saw none of it," said Bunny Wailer when he heard about the payments.

During the nine months Bob had been in Wilmington, two events of considerable significance had taken place in Jamaica.

On the music front, the ska beat, which up to then had been a staple of the Wailers' repertoire and which had ruled Jamaica for more than half a decade, had been overtaken during the sweltering summer of 1966 by a slower, heavier, more sensual rhythm called rock steady. The dominant horns of the ska era were either pushed into the background or disappeared entirely, with the rhythmic emphasis coming from the heart-pounding drum and bass, a combination that would soon become the foundation of the next step in Jamaica's musical evolution: the marginally faster reggae.

It was a sound the Wailers, always innovative and experimental, embraced enthusiastically and, with their fledgling Wail N Soul M label giving them more artistic freedom than they'd ever experienced, they were to record some of their most significant work during the two years of the rock-steady era.

Bob, as usual, had his own take on what was happening. He told one reporter that "the guys who were in control robbed the older musicians up, and they get frustrated and stop playing. So the musicians changed from the older musicians to the younger, hungrier ones who was coming up underneath them . . . We don't want to stand around playing and singing that ska beat any more. The young musicians, dem have a different beat. It was rock steady now, ready to go."

With Bob back as lead vocalist, the Wailers recorded gem after gem during the rock-steady era, usually at West Indies Studio, a four-track facility at 15 Bell Road in Kingston owned by an entrepreneur with political aspirations called Edward Seaga and soon to be taken over by the popular band leader Byron Lee and renamed Dynamic Sound.

Among the classics on the Wail N Soul M label in that era were "Nice Time," "Hypocrites," "Mellow Mood," "Stir It Up," and "Don't Rock My Boat" (all with Bob on lead vocal), and "Hammer," "Stepping Razor," and "Mus' Get a Beatin'" (all with Peter on lead vocal or sharing lead vocals with Bob).

Even though money was still tight and they were funding the sessions themselves, it's interesting to note that the Wailers continued to record with the cream of Jamaican studio musicians. Among the stalwarts who accompanied them frequently during the rock-steady era were Hugh Malcolm on drums, Jackie Jackson on bass, Winston Wright and Gladstone Anderson on keyboards, Lyn Taitt on guitar, and Skatalites veterans Tommy McCook and Roland Alphonso on saxophone and "Dizzy" Johnny Moore on trumpet.

The other event of major significance during 1966 was the visit to Jamaica of the man the rapidly growing Rastafarian movement on the island worshipped as a living god: His Imperial Majesty Haile Selassie I of Ethiopia.

For months before the 21 April arrival of their beloved Jah, excitement had mounted in Rastafarian communities throughout the island, and tens of thousands of dreadlocked believers started converging on Kingston days and even weeks before the momentous day, many of them setting up makeshift camps on the narrow strip of land known as the Palisadoes that leads to Kingston's international airport and, eventually, the town of Port Royal, once a pirate haven known as "the wickedest place on earth."

The story of what happened on that historic day has been told many times: how the mounting excitement exploded into near hysteria when Selassie's plane broke through the clouds and started its descent, and how thousands of Rastafarians, unable to contain themselves or to let themselves be contained, broke through police lines and swarmed around the plane, openly smoking their chalices and chanting hymns and psalms. Selassie, taken totally by surprise, took a quick look at the chaos surrounding his plane, ordered the doors shut, and refused to emerge for an hour until Kingston's most prominent Rasta elder, Mortimer Planno, managed to persuade the excited crowd to make some room so the man they adored and revered could set foot on their island.

It was a day such as Jamaica's Rastafarians, disdained or looked upon with suspicion by the majority of the island's population, had never experienced. Brother George Huggins of Accompong, the semi-autonomous Maroon community deep in the Jamaican hinterland, explained the ecstatic welcome this way: "It is hard to put in words what seeing this man, this great man, the Lord of Lords, in Jamaica meant to us in the Rastafarian community. We had heard so much about him for so long."

Bob Marley, who had become increasingly drawn to the Rastafarian movement before leaving for Wilmington, wasn't there to see it. But his new wife was, and through her eyewitness account the events of that day were to have a profound impact on the rest of his life. Rita Marley had been one of the multitude who'd set off on foot from Trench Town to greet Selassie at the airport, but when she and some friends arrived in the vicinity of the huge cement works on the left-hand side of the road leading from Kingston to the Palisadoes peninsula they decided that they'd halt there and wait for Selassie's motorcade, which would have to pass that spot on its way into the capital.

Rita had set out that morning with a firm plan in her head—and it wasn't simply to see Selassie in the flesh. She was still a Christian, but she had heard that Selassie had a stigmata—nail-prints of the Crucifixion—in his palms. Like Bob, she had been drawn toward the Rastafarian religion and way of life but she remained a little skeptical. If she could see the nailprints, she told herself, she too would be convinced that Haile Selassie was a living god. With Selassie's motorcade approaching, Rita watched anxiously, waiting for some sort of sign. And, as it flashed past, she got one. Selassie, she told Bob excitedly on his return to Jamaica six months later, had caught her eye and waved to her. And she'd seen the stigmata.

That was enough for Rita Marley. From that moment, she embraced the Rastafarian movement wholeheartedly.

And when she told Bob the story, it reinforced his already strong feelings toward Rastafari. He'd already started to let his hair grow into short locks—to his mother's chagrin—during his last few months in Delaware, and with Rita's powerful story adding to his growing convictions he sought out Mortimer Planno, whom he knew from Trench Town, to seek advice and guidance about the Rastafarian religion and way of life.

Planno, although unquestionably a leading member of Jamaica's Rastafarian movement, was always a controversial figure, and many people in the reggae world have questioned his motivations and his honesty. One thing that is known for certain about him is that he recognized an opportunity when he saw one—and he saw one in Bob Marley. For a while, Planno assumed the role of Bob's Rastafarian mentor, instructing him in his sepulchral voice about the history and intricacies of the movement, and at the same time playing an increasingly important—some would say insidious —role in the management of the Wailers, whose other members were by now also wholly committed Rastafarians.

Bob's eyes were also being opened to the harsh realities of the record business. The money he'd put into the Wail N Soul M venture had been enough for the Wailers to produce their own records, but insufficient to market and sell them as efficiently as the big studios, and, once again, times were tough for Bob, Rita, and young Sharon, who Bob was to adopt and whom he always treated as his own daughter.

With Rita by now pregnant, the couple decided they'd be better off living in Nine Mile. In Kingston, Bob was under so much pressure he was suffering from writer's block, and many of those who were close to him at the time say he was also determined to distance himself from Planno, with whom he'd become increasingly disillusioned and who was also viewed with considerable suspicion by both Bunny and Peter.

Bob Marley felt he needed to get back to his roots, to be a simple farmer again.

Omeriah Malcolm had passed away in 1965, and the tiny wooden house he'd built for Cedella two decades earlier was vacant. The young family moved into it, and with Bob back in the familiar surroundings of his childhood, they quickly settled in. For Rita, who'd been a city girl all her life, the move was a particularly momentous one. "It was different for me, because I'd never been exposed to the country. I had to carry water, collect wood to make the fire, and I had to sleep on a little bed on the dirt because they didn't have flooring. But it was all out of love. I had decided to do so, and it didn't matter. I was going into the faith of Rastafari, and I was seeking to find an independent sort of self. Because Bob was already exposed to this lifestyle, it was a thrill for him to see me just living it.

"We did a lot of writing and singing there, sharing a lot of special times, special moments. I was getting to know the other side of him, more so than just being in the studio. He'd try out stuff on me—listen to this one, listen to that one. And look up into the sky and air . . . A lot of inspiration coming from there."

While they were living in Nine Mile, Bob would commute frequently to Kingston for recording sessions and to take care of Wail N Soul M business. The sessions went well enough. But the business side of Wail N Soul M didn't get any better. "We were too young for producing," Peter Tosh said years later. "We never understood certain important things, like how to get on the air or sell our records. We only knew how to make them."

It soon became clear to the Wailers that their first venture into the perilous waters of the record business wasn't about to become the financial success they'd hoped and worked for, even if it brought significant contributions to their expanding body of work. They needed help, and with a growing family—Rita had given birth to Cedella, named after Bob's mother, on 23 August 1967— Bob continued to seek guidance and inspiration from Rastafari. During his frequent trips from Nine Mile to Kingston, he had become a regular participant at Rasta "grounations," which consisted mainly of hours of impassioned drumming and chanting and ganja-induced meditation. It was at one of these grounations, very early in 1968, that Bob Marley had another of the fateful encounters that would influence the direction of his life.

He met an American pop-soul singer called Johnny Nash.

6.
The Night Shift

Today Johnny Nash is best remembered for the material he recorded in Jamaica or in a reggae-esque vein, much of it either written by Bob Marley or co-written by the two of them. The biggest single hit of his highly successful career, "I Can See Clearly Now," is a reggae ballad, and in the early seventies he had considerable chart success with Wailers' standards like "Stir It Up" and "Mellow Mood."

But in 1968, when he first met Bob, Nash was internationally known for his somewhat sanitized "soul" recordings, which brought him commercial success but which, to his chagrin, sold mainly to a white audience. He had also landed starring roles in a couple of Hollywood movies, called *Take a Giant Step* and *Key Witness*. He was a highly marketable showbiz commodity when he teamed up with an ambitious promoter called Danny Sims in New York, and Sims organized a successful Caribbean tour for Nash in the early sixties. Early in 1967, as their friendship grew closer and their business dealings prospered, Sims and Nash decided to move their operational base to Jamaica.

Later that year, accompanied by their producer, Arthur Jenkins, Sims and Nash flew into Kingston with the intention of absorbing some of the island's exciting music vibes and cutting some records in a country where costs were considerably below those in New York. In Kingston, Nash soon recorded an album called *Hold Me Tight*, which sold briskly internationally and featured a reggae-infused version of the Sam Cooke classic "Cupid."

From the beginning Nash enjoyed living and working in Jamaica. The music scene could hardly have been more vibrant, with ska having been overtaken by the newer, slower, heavier rock-steady beat—infinitely more suited to his superb tenor voice than the faster, jerkier tempo of its predecessor. In addition, crime and violence were virtually non-existent by today's standards and usually confined to the sort of areas a visitor to the island wouldn't frequent.

As he fell into the laid-back Jamaican way of life, Nash soon became fascinated by a group of people unlike any he'd encountered in his life: the Rastafarians. He was determined to find out more about them, and about the heartbeat music that was one of the foundation-stones of their movement. He was invited— something of a rarity for an outsider—to attend a Rasta grounation. He was taken there by a well-known Jamaican broadcaster he'd befriended, Neville Willoughby, and at the grounation he was introduced to a young Rastafarian and fellow musician who told him his name was Bob Marley.

The following day Nash introduced his new friend to Danny Sims, and they listened, transfixed, as Marley sang song after song after song for them—all, as Sims was to recall years later, potential hits. It was the start of a long musical association, although it was to be one that seldom resulted in the artistic or commercial success that had been anticipated.

Sims, Nash, and Jenkins formed a new label, JAD Records, named for Johnny, Arthur, and Danny, and signed a songwriting contract with the Wailers. Bob, Bunny, and Peter were to cut many tracks for them over the next three to four years, and were reportedly paid $50 a week each, a considerable amount in those days. But while their new producers may have been more generous than Clement Dodd, they had nothing like Coxson's feel for the music of Jamaica, and the late sixties were mainly a confusing and frustrating period in the careers of the three Wailers.

Bob was more or less commuting between his idyllic rural life in Nine Mile and recording occasionally in Kingston; Bunny was serving a year in prison on ganja charges he swears were false; Peter, frustrated by years of business chicanery, was utilizing his guitar skills by hiring himself out as a session musician, for which he was in considerable demand and for which he actually received money (session players were paid by the track, rather than having to wait for royalty payments that rarely materialized).

The first Danny Sims-produced tracks by the Wailers, minus the incarcerated Bunny and with Peter and Rita Marley singing harmony behind Bob's lead vocals, were recorded in Sims's rented house in Kingston in late January 1968. The tracks, none written by the Wailers, all shallow and trite by their standards and not released until many years later, were "Fallin' In and Out of Love," "Stranger on the Shore," "Splish for My Splash," the traditional "Wings of a Dove," and "Want Love True Love."

A few months later many of the same tracks were recorded by the group, again at Sims's house. Again, not one was released until years later (so many years, in fact, that there was time for three of Bob's sons, Stephen, Damian, and Julian, all still to be born in 1968, to contribute additional harmony vocals).

Between these two sessions the group continued, doggedly, to turn out self-produced material on Wail N Soul M, most of it with Peter and Bob sharing lead vocals and Rita helping out on harmony during Bunny's absence. The fact that these Wail N Soul M sessions produced some of the rarest Wailers tracks ever recorded, and the fact that the legion of avid Wailers collectors around the world have never managed to lay their hands on at least two of them, while many of the others have been tracked down only in pre-release form with handwritten titles on blank labels, are probably accurate indications of how the label's marketing and retailing was functioning at the time.

Soon after the second session in Sims's Russell Heights home, in the more professional surroundings of Randy's Studio, and with Rita again replacing the still-absent Bunny on harmony vocal, the group recorded some considerably more substantial material: "Nice Time," "Bend Down Low," and "Soul Almighty." Another successful session followed soon after, this time a vastly different version of the classic "Mellow Mood." Next, at a September session at West Indies Studio, came the first recording of a song that was to become another Wailers classic, "Soul Rebel." The fact that virtually nothing is known about this landmark session—apart from the fact Bob was singing lead—is another indication of the uncertainty of that era.

Late in 1968, with Bunny by now out of prison and back with the group, the title of one of the tracks recorded at another West Indies Studio session says it all about the artistic compromises the greatest harmony trio in Jamaica were having to make: it was called "Milkshake and Potato Chips."

The Wailers needed a change, and Bob figured that to bring about change they needed money so they could again have a label of their own. Almost three years had passed since he'd found himself in a virtually identical situation, when the Wailers decided they'd finally had enough of their relationship with Coxson Dodd. And this time Bob came to the same conclusion—he'd have to go to the States and save enough money to kick-start the Wailers' by-now erratic career.

Although it had been far from satisfactory, the Wailers' association with Nash and Sims—with whom they had a composing and performing contract—was by no means over, and the two Americans were again to figure prominently in their careers, particularly Bob's, before too long. In the spring of 1969—he'd learned the hard way about Delaware winters—Bob Marley again set off for Wilmington, where his mother, Cedella, and her Mr. Booker now had a son, Richard, born not long after Bob had left Delaware late in 1966.

This time, Bob didn't leave Rita in Jamaica. She was with him on the flight, along with their daughter Cedella, by now a toddler, and baby David, known to everyone as Ziggy, who had been born on 17 October 1968.

The long flight with several stopovers and two restless children took its toll on Bob and Rita, and this reunion wasn't as joyous as past ones had been. Cedella's main recollection of it is that the weary couple were snapping at each other virtually from the moment they arrived, and that she and Mr. Booker drove them to Wilmington as quickly as possible so they could get some much-needed sleep. The real reunion took place the following morning, and Bob and Rita were soon looking for jobs. Rita found one as a housekeeper, and Bob got a job on the night shift on the assembly line at a Chrysler factory, where he drove a fork lift and which inspired one of his most famous compositions, "Night Shift."

The Wailers would record the song under the title "It's Alright" the following year, but it wasn't until 1976 that "Night Shift" was introduced to the world, by now eagerly awaiting every Bob Marley recording, on *Rastaman Vibration*, which was to be the only Marley album to make the top ten in the American charts during his lifetime.

Apart from getting the inspiration for "Night Shift" and practicing whenever he had a spare minute, Bob had to deal with his new family responsibilities during his second stay in Wilmington, and Cedella recalls frequent quarrels between him and Rita. "Sometimes they would fuss and I'd hear Rita wailing upstairs and go up to see what was the matter, but always they would quiet down when they heard my footsteps."

There was also an incident that, according to Cedella, Rita has never forgotten or quite forgiven her for. It came when Bob, always a notoriously stern and uncompromising musical taskmaster, was rehearsing a new number in Cedella's drawing room, with his wife and mother contributing backing vocals. Rita, despite being an experienced and accomplished singer, couldn't hit the notes Bob wanted, and, says Cedella, he became more and more exasperated with her, prompting the older woman to remark, somewhat mischievously, "Rita, me never know you can't sing."

Bob also made some new friends in Wilmington—and it was to them he made the ominous prediction that he would die young.

Ibis Pitts and his wife Genny first met Bob Marley in their gift shop in Wilmington. They recall a shy young man who helped them to make wire jewellery, some of which Ibis took to sell at the legendary Woodstock rock festival in upstate New York. They also recall Bob's copious ganja consumption and his skill in handling the bounty of an eight-foot-tall marijuana plant he had been growing in Cedella's and Mr. Booker's back garden.

Musicologist and reggae archivist Roger Steffens interviewed Ibis Pitts for the Bob Marley Collectors' Edition he edits annually for *The Beat*, the authoritative Los Angeles-based reggae and world beat magazine. This is Pitts's description of Bob's fluency with his beloved herb:

> He went out there and tore off a whole bunch, green, and came back to the house with it, put some in a pan with some water in it, and put it on a stove and boiled it a little bit. It turned a real pretty green. He put it in a cup and put a little honey in it, and it was so good. I had never heard of that before. And he put another big handful of green between a newspaper and ironed it on his mother's ironing board, instantly drying it, and rolled it in some papers. BOMB!

Not all of Ibis's memories of Bob were so lighthearted. He was there when his new friend made the prediction that—tragically— would become one of his most famous. Ibis, Bob, and another friend, Dion Wilson, were hanging out in the gift shop when Dion told Bob, who wasn't enjoying the night shift at Chrysler, that he was destined to become rich, famous, and live a long and happy life. "Oh, no, I'm going to die at thirty-six," Marley said earnestly.

Ibis and Dion didn't take the young musician's premonition too seriously. But twelve years later, recalls Ibis, "When he [Dion] heard the news about Nesta passing, he said, 'Nesta said he was going to be leaving at thirty-six.' And I said, 'Wow, yeah, Dion.'"

Before long, Bob decided it was time to return to Jamaica. The second Delaware trip hadn't been a huge success financially —there were more mouths to feed this time round—but he figured he had enough for the Wailers to start producing their own music again. In late 1969, leaving Rita and the kids in Wilmington, Bob flew back to Kingston.

The Wailers were eager to resume their career. The rock-steady era had run its course, and the music ruling Jamaica—and starting to make an impact worldwide—was reggae. A shade faster than rock steady but with the same emphasis on the bass and drums as its rhythmic anchor, reggae had burst onto the Jamaican scene in 1968 with a Leslie Kong-produced song called "Do the Reggay" by Toots and the Maytals, veterans from the ska era, fronted by the gospel-fueled vocals of the great Frederick "Toots" Hibbert, a singer whowould undoubtedly have been a soul superstar of Otis Redding stature had he been American, and who was to carve out a legendary career in reggae that would endure well into the next millennium.

Desmond Dekker, Bob's old friend from his welding days, had recorded a huge international hit, "Israelites," and was in England making guest appearances on the British program *Top of the Pops*, in those days one of the trendiest yardsticks anywhere of what was hot in the pop music world.

Reggae was happening—but the Wailers weren't, and Bob, Bunny, and Peter were determined that this would change. Their collective return to the studio, however, was less than an instant success.

They desperately tried to come up with a winning formula, recording a self-produced, thinly disguised cover version of James Brown's US monster "Say It Loud I'm Black and Proud," titled "Black Progress," which sounded forced and jerky. The Wailers may have been big fans of the Godfather of Soul, but none of their voices came close to matching Brown's raw vocal power, and when they tried the strain showed. Recorded at Randy's Studio 17, this session was historic despite any shortcomings of the actual music: it was the first time the three Wailers were backed by the drum and bass masters Aston and Carlton Barrett, who were to become permanent members of the group and who would play a pivotal role in Bob's recording and touring in the years ahead.

Worse was to come, in the shape of cover versions of the Archies' "Sugar Sugar," a saccharine kiddy-pop hit in the States, and the Box Tops' "Give Me a Ticket," an equally asinine US chart smash.

In the early summer of 1970, the frustrated and ever-broke Wailers decided to accept an offer from the man who had put out Bob's first singles in 1962 and who had become the island's most successful producer in the late sixties: Leslie Kong. By now, Kong was on top of the heap in the fiercely competitive world of Jamaican music. He'd produced Desmond Dekker's monster hit "Israelites" and several other Dekker UK chart successes, among them the hypnotically catchy "It Mek" and the superb "007 (Shanty Town)," and the roster of artists working for him included

JA chart regulars like Ken Boothe, Delroy Wilson, and the Melodians.

Kong's label, Beverley's, was a hit-making machine almost on a par with Coxson Dodd's, and, like Dodd, he used the island's finest session musicians, always an important consideration for the Wailers, even when they were down on their luck.

On 5 May 1970, Bob, Bunny, and Peter found themselves back at 15 Bell Road in the familiar surroundings of the old West Indies Records studio, which had recently been bought by band leader Byron Lee and renamed Dynamic Sounds.

They returned to the studio twice in the following weeks, and before May was out they'd recorded all the tracks for a complete album, among them "Caution," "Soul Captives," "Soul Shakedown Party," "Cheer Up," and "Soon Come."

The bright, bouncy sound that was Kong's trademark and that epitomized reggae in those early days was a distinct improvement on some of the material the Wailers had been putting out over the past year or so, but Bob, Peter, and Bunny were horrified when Kong told them he was going to call their soon-to-be-released album "The Best of the Wailers."

Bunny was particularly vehement in his opposition, telling Kong angrily that it was wrong to call something "the best of" when the young group clearly had a long career ahead of them, and warning, ominously, that "if this is our best to you, it must mean that you are at the end of your life."

It's not known if Bunny uttered those words in patois or the deep, deliberate, meticulously enunciated speech he reserves for pronouncements of special import, but it is known that Kong ignored him and the other members of the group and put the album on the market with the title he'd chosen.

On 9 April 1971, Kong was in the studio soon after recording Jimmy Cliff's tracks for Perry Henzell's seminal movie *The Harder They Come*. Kong, who was just thirty-eight and had no known history of coronary problems, suffered a massive heart attack and died instantly.

The Wailers continued to record sporadically in the months following their Leslie Kong sessions, but their music, always eclectic, lacked any real direction or consistency.

They were in dire need of new musical guidance. All they were looking for was a producer who could inspire and challenge them artistically, find them studio time with the top musicians they insisted on working with, and pay them what they believed they were worth.

Enter Lee "Scratch" Perry—and two out of three isn't bad.

Lee "Scratch" Perry: reggae's eccentric genius produced some of the Wailers' finest work. Perry ranks second only to Coxson Dodd as the most influential producer in reggae history.

7.
Scratch and Beyond

L ee "Scratch" Perry could be fairly and accurately described as: a creative genius; a reggae pioneer; a master of the mixing board; a shrewd businessman; a superb singer; a gifted and imaginative songwriter; a compelling stage performer; a talent-spotter with an unerring ear; a monumental figure in the evolution of Jamaican music.

There are also those who say he's stark raving mad.

There's a considerable amount of evidence to support all of the above, although many veteran observers of the reggae scene have long suspected that Perry's sometimes bizarre behavior—he may be the only record producer in history to have deliberately burned down his own studio—is merely eccentric, rather than lunatic. For someone whose sanity has been questioned so frequently over the years, Perry hasn't done too badly. Check the reggae bins at any major CD store, and chances are that next to Bob Marley and the Wailers, Perry will be the artist with the biggest selection. An inveterate globe-trotter—over the past couple of decades, he's lived in England, the Netherlands, Switzerland, (where he married a millionairess, hardly the hallmark of insanity) and Jamaica. Rainford Hugh Perry was born in Hanover, Jamaica, in 1936, and his music career started in the late fifties, when he was hired by Coxson Dodd, who had just started to produce his own records, to organize studio sessions, scout for new talent, and supervise auditions.

By 1963 he was writing songs for some of Dodd's leading performers, including the Maytals and Delroy Wilson, and also releasing the first of his own recordings, in the ska tempo that was ruling Jamaica at the time. One of these singles, "Chicken Scratch," earned him the most famous of his many nicknames.

It was at Dodd's Studio One that Perry first met Bob Marley, Peter Tosh, and Bunny Wailer, and they collaborated on one of his early 45s for Coxsone, recording an obscure single called "Man to Man" in 1964 with Scratch on lead vocals, Bob, Bunny, Peter, and Junior Braithwaite singing harmony, and backed by the Skatalites. (The intro was similar, but this wasn't the same "Man to Man" the Wailers were to record with Perry six years later.)

The small but scrappy Perry had a falling out with Coxson in 1967 and left to begin working with other producers, notably Clancy Eccles and Joe Gibbs. He teamed up with Gibbs in 1968 to produce "The Upsetter," a musical attack on Dodd that earned him his next nickname, "Upsetter." Later that year, Perry parted company with Gibbs, and immediately launched an even more vitriolic musical attack on his most recent partner, "People Funny Boy." It was a hit in Jamaica, a nation with a historic taste for a good vendetta, particularly when you can dance to it.

Perry, perhaps beginning to realize he wasn't destined to work for anybody but himself, started his own Upsetter label in 1968, and quickly recruited a small but formidable team of studio musicians. The core members were Glen Adams on keyboards, Alva "Reggie" Lewis on guitar, Aston "Family Man" Barrett on bass, and his younger brother, Carlton, on drums. They had played gigs together as the Hippy Boys and the Reggae Boys, usually with Max Romeo on lead vocals, but for studio purposes Scratch renamed them the Upsetters.

The label was an immediate success, with hits by David Isaacs and the Untouchables, and Perry soon signed a contract with Trojan, the main distributor of Jamaican music in the UK at the time. The following year, 1969, Perry was riding high on the mainstream British charts with the Upsetters' "The Return of Django," which reached No. 5 and stayed there for three weeks. On the strength of it, the band toured England.

In 1974, with more than a hundred singles on the Upsetter label behind him, Perry decided it was time to open his own studio. He built it in the backyard of his home at 5 Cardiff Crescent in Kingston, and he called it Black Ark. He was to burn it down six years later, but not before it had been the source of some of the greatest reggae ever recorded.

Perry's timing couldn't have been better: Black Ark was born in the infancy of what is now remembered, almost reverently, as the roots reggae era and, inevitably, Perry had a huge hit soon after the four-track studio opened for business—Junior Byles's classic "Curly Locks." And the hits kept on coming. Among them were Susan Cadogan's "Hurts So Good," which climbed to No. 4 on the UK charts; Junior Murvin's monster "Police and Thieves," also a UK chart hit; Max Romeo's "War ina Babylon"; George Faith's "To Be a Lover," and the Heptones' "Party Time," a number the seminal roots trio had also recorded years earlier at Studio One.

Perry also produced a slew of legendary albums, among them the Congos' *Heart of the Congos*, the Upsetters' *Super Ape*, the Cimarons' *On the Rock,* and a virtually unknown classic called *Conscious Man* by a sadly under-recorded and under-appreciated harmony trio, the Jolly Boys.

However oddball his behavior could be, there's not the slightest doubt that Lee "Scratch" Perry is a shoo-in for instant inclusion in any reggae hall of fame, and it was to this diminutive genius that the Wailers turned in 1970.

The previous two or three years hadn't been vintage ones for Bob, Bunny, or Peter. As usual, they were broke most of the time. And since their split from Coxson in 1966 they'd been inconsistent musically, with a few flashes of brilliance in the midst of what was mostly the least memorable output of their careers. It hadn't helped that Bunny's crucial harmonies and spiritual guidance had been missing for the year he spent in jail, that Bob had been absent for even longer, cumulatively, during his two trips to Wilmington, and that Peter had been forced to pick up session work wherever he could to put bread on the table and help finance what the group hoped would be their imminent return to producing their own music.

They prayed their luck would change when they linked up with Lee Perry in 1970, a few months after Bob's return from his second trip to Wilmington. They hoped that the maverick producer, brimming with new ideas and new hard sounds, with his own label and a solid track record of hits, would put their careers back on track; that they'd be on the charts again and that this time round they'd be properly compensated for their work.

Artistically, at least, their prayers were answered.

Lee Perry took them back to their roots, back to the days when they were the musical embodiment of the rude-boy era, back to the not-so-long-ago days when they were the hottest group on the Jamdown charts, back to the days when they were the simmer-down darlings of the sound systems, back to sounding dread.

To Scratch, the drum and bass were what made reggae tick. Throw in keyboards and a choppy, chugging, almost metronomic guitar, all but forget about the horns that had played such a huge role in ska, put him at the controls, and the result was guaranteed to be the tightest, baddest reggae that had ever assailed the eardrums of Jamaica.

He wasted no time in reinventing the Wailers' sound, dropping the doo-wop style harmonies that had been one of their trademarks, and encouraging them to follow their own musical instincts. "We come from Trench Town," Bob was to sing almost a decade later. In 1970, Scratch reminded the Wailers of that.

The group's first recordings with Perry were at Dynamic Sounds in August 1970. The tracks, "My Cup" and "Try Me," were fine, but they gave only the slightest indication of the musical renaissance that was just around the corner.

It arrived the following month, when the group returned to 15 Bell Road for historic sessions that yielded the first versions of two songs that were to become Wailers classics: "Small Axe" and "Duppy Conqueror." They were a revelation. You could skank to them, but they were also a touch menacing, drawing on ghetto imagery and thinly disguised threats— "If you are a big tree, we are a small axe, sharpened to cut you down," sang Bob on "Small Axe." The warning wasn't directed at some inoffensive banyan tree—in Jamaican patois, the word "three" comes out sounding like "tree," and "Small Axe" served notice on the three giants of the Jamaican recording industry of that era—Studio One, Federal, and Dynamic Sounds—that their stranglehold was about to be broken.

The Wailers were wailin' again.

The first version of another landmark Wailers song was also recorded at those early Lee Perry sessions. "Man to Man" (later retitled and better known as "Who the Cap Fit" from the 1976 *Rastaman Vibration* album) showed an emerging side of Bob Marley's songwriting. Like Rita, Bunny, and Peter, Bob was by now heavily committed to Rastafari. The Bible was a bedrock of their beliefs, and Bob was starting to draw more and more heavily on it, sometimes directly, sometimes with subtle paraphrasing, sometimes simply as the source of inspiration, in many of his compositions.

In the past, while the Wailers had no qualms about addressing social issues, these were mainly of a somewhat parochial nature—dispensing warnings and advice to rampaging rude boys or lamenting the hypocrites in their midst. With "Man to Man," the target audience was much, much broader. "Man to man is so unjust, children you don't know who to trust," sang Bob. They were words that couldn't help strike a chord with anyone who'd lived on our troubled planet.

Magic was in the air, but the musicians were so busy making it happen they didn't realize it. "After more than twenty years, I finally started to appreciate it. Back then I didn't know," Glen Adams, the keyboard player for those historic sessions, told an interviewer almost a quarter-century later.

In November 1970, Perry took the Wailers back into the studio —this time Randy's Studio 17. There, they recorded "Soul Rebel," with Bob singing lead, and Peter's "400 Years." The Wailers ended 1970 buoyantly, and started 1971 on an even higher note.

Their first session of the new year, again at Randy's Studio 17, was one of the most historic in the story of popular music. The only song they tackled that day was called "Kaya"— a Jamaican word for marijuana—and it featured some of the most sensuous, sinuous vocals Bob Marley would ever record. At the same session, they also recorded "Kaya Version," with Bob launching into almost ethereal scat. He was singing as he'd never sung before, and his voice, although never powerful in the classical sense, was by now so flexible he could do virtually anything he wanted with it. The countless hours he'd spent in Joe Higgs's and Tata's yards, in Coxson's studio, in Cedella's home in Wilmington, and just about everywhere else he'd had the chance to master his chosen profession, were paying serious dividends. He'd always been able to sing. Now, although he could hardly have known it at the time, he could sing better than anyone else in the world.

The master works kept on coming. The Kaya session was followed, almost immediately, by another in which the Wailers recorded a medley of some of their biggest hits in one 45 rpm single—an almost dizzying phantasmagoria of melodies that before long would be recognized as some of the greatest of the twentieth century. The brainchild of Lee Perry, it featured snatches of "Bend Down Low," "Nice Time," "One Love," "Simmer Down," "It Hurts to Be Alone," "Lonesome Feelings," "Love and Affection," "Put It On," and "Duppy Conqueror."

Other classics followed in quick succession, among them "Keep on Moving," "African Herbsman," "Fussing and Fighting," and "Stand Alone."

As well as churning out a steady stream of well-received 45s, Perry packaged the Wailers' prodigious output from this brief but intense era into two albums, *Soul Rebels* and *Soul Revolution*. To this day, many long-time Wailers fans are convinced that the group's work with Lee Perry was the finest of their careers. A third album, *African Herbsman*, containing many of the very best of the songs from these sessions, was also put together by Perry. It's arguably the single greatest album ever by the Wailers . . . and until they came across it in a store in England some time later they didn't know it existed.

The sound Perry coaxed from the Wailers might have been substantially different from their Coxson days, but the two shrewd producers did have one thing in common—an almost pathological aversion to paying the musicians who were making them wealthy.

The Wailers were back on the JA charts, and their records were hugely popular with the West Indian community in England. But they were still broke. Years later Bunny Wailer recalled those days bitterly: "We never made a dime from any of them. Perry refused to give us our money when it came time for us to collect. He said he had decided to just give us some royalties. But we have never seen anything at all. Nothing. Not one penny."

Inevitably, the group's relationship with Perry became strained, and various accounts of physical violence between them have surfaced over the years. There are tales of Bob and Scratch getting into frequent altercations, presumably in the bantamweight division; and of the Wailers beating up Perry so badly he had to be hospitalized. There were no known witnesses to that alleged incident, and the thought of the three tough young Wailers, by now completely immersed in the spiritual beliefs of Rastafari, ganging up on the tiny Scratch is almost too preposterous to contemplate seriously.

As the Wailers' frustrations with Perry mounted, Bob was becoming close friends with Jamaica's most famous soccer player, Alan "Skill" Cole. Skill had played for one of the world's great club teams, Brazil's Santos, and was the most idolized sports figure in Jamaica. He was an avid music fan. Bob was crazy about soccer. They also had a shared belief in Rastafari, and a love of ganja and physical fitness. Cole reputedly had links with some of Kingston's criminal elements, and many believe that a scam-gone-wrong in which he might have been involved was the reason Bob Marley almost lost his life in 1976.

Cole encouraged the Wailers to set up their own label, and in March 1971, in a co-production with Scratch, the group recorded a song called "Send Me That Love." It was the first session that would produce a single on the now legendary Tuff Gong label. That same month the Wailers, still in an uneasy partnership with Scratch, returned to Randy's Studio 17 to record the earliest versions of songs that were to become classics, among them "Sun Is Shining" and "Don't Rock My Boat."

These co-produced sessions were the last the Wailers would

record in partnership with Lee Perry—at least for a while; he was to pop up again, as feisty and brilliant as ever, a few years down the line in Bob's career.

The Wailers may not have made much money from their association with Scratch, but they didn't come out of it entirely empty-handed: they took the guts of Perry's great Upsetters band with them. Just playing with the Wailers had been a thrill for Aston and Carlton Barrett, who'd been huge fans of the group since their "Simmer Down" days. And when the Wailers parted company with Perry, "Family Man" and "Carly" decided to go with them.

"Bob is the leader of the Wailers, and I am the leader of the musical part of the group," says Fams. "The Wailers was the best vocal group and I group was the best little backing band at the time, so we say, why don't we just come together and mosh up the world."

Aston "Family Man" Barrett, now universally revered as the greatest bass player in the history of reggae music—the man who created and played the bass lines that anchored and redefined the sound of Bob Marley and the Wailers throughout the seventies—was born in Kingston in 1946. He was always fascinated by music, and like countless other Jamaican youngsters he soon started building his own instruments. The first instrument he made was a makeshift bass guitar. As he told an interviewer in 1975, "I build my own bass. I build one out of board and I put on four string. I don't go to school, you know, no one teach I."

No one needed to. Aston Barrett had an affinity for the bass guitar that many believe to be unmatched in the history of popular music. There have undoubtedly been bass players with quicker fingers, more virtuoso skills, more flash, than Family Man. But there's never been anyone who could create and play a more rock-solid, penetrating, deadly bass pattern. And, as the years were to prove, he could do it virtually ad infinitum. For every sublime melody Bob Marley was to come up with, Family Man would invent the perfect bass line to complement it.

Before long, he became the undisputed No. 2 in the Wailers' hierarchy, second only to Bob himself, and the sole commander when it came to that crucial bass: "The bass is the root. You've got

Bass master: Aston "Family Man" Barrett

to have a strong foundation . . . Family Man take care of the bass
. . . Family Man controls reggae," Bob Marley would tell an interviewer in 1975.

The other half of the formidable rhythm section that the Wailers
snatched from Scratch was Family Man's younger brother. Carlton
"Carly" Barrett, creator of the "One Drop" sound, was born in
Kingston in 1950. Drawn toward drums rather than guitar, he used
paint cans to make his first instruments, and he was still a teenager
when he started playing professionally as a member of the Hippy Boys.

As a youngster, he was inspired by the drumming of the Skatalites' Lloyd Nibbs, and as reggae evolved and the Wailers soared to
superstardom his sometimes driving, sometimes delicate drumming,
locked in perfect tandem with big brother Fams's spine-bending bass,
was at the heart of their world-conquering sound.

The "Rock My Boat" and "Sun Is Shining" sessions at Randy's
had been an encouraging start to the Wailers' Tuff Gong venture,
but not encouraging enough to prevent the ambitious young Bob
Marley from accepting an offer from Danny Sims to go to Sweden.

Johnny Nash was there to star in and record the music for a movie to be called *Want So Much To Believe*. Sims and Nash wanted Bob to help with the soundtrack, and in the spring of 1971 he joined them in the Swedish capital of Stockholm.

Bob was to spend almost three months in Sweden. The trip wasn't a complete waste of time, but it wasn't far short of it.

Marley had spent the previous year on a creative high, making new and vibrant music in a familiar environment and surrounded by familiar faces. In Sweden, he found himself in a world that was colder in more ways than one.

Johnny Nash had rented a house in Nockeby, about six miles outside Stockholm, and surrounded himself with an eclectic mix of musicians, who were working with him on the movie sound-track. Among them were John "Rabbit" Bundrick, a talented young keyboard player from Texas, the up-and-coming Swedish guitarist Jan Schaffer, and three other European session musicians.

Bob Marley became part of this musical smorgasbord in late March. His welcome wasn't particularly encouraging. For one thing, with the exception of Johnny Nash, no one could decipher his Jamaican patois. And, not knowing a thing about reggae at the time, they were skeptical about his competence.

"Rabbit" Bundrick, who was to work closely with Bob a couple of years later on the Wailers' breakthrough album *Catch a Fire*, recalls: "This was the first time I met Bob Marley and I thought, 'Oh my God, this will never work! He can't even tune his guitar and I can't understand a word he says.'"

Marley quickly picked up on the negative vibes. He had been allocated a small room in the basement of the rented house, and for the first part of his stay he kept to himself. Bundrick's Swedish girl-friend, Marlene Lingard, was spending a lot of time at the house and the studio, and she remembers Bob living almost as a recluse in his basement room, "just to be alone and stay away from the others. He was sulking a lot and playing his guitar . . . When he was in his better moods, he cooked for us and introduced us to fish tea and other exotic foods."

One incident in particular illustrates how out of sorts Bob Marley must have been at the time.

The Nockeby house was a musicians' hangout, almost a commune, and there were always attractive young women hanging around. The withdrawn and reclusive Marley was in the shower one morning when he suddenly found himself joined by a girl as naked as he was. Lars Rossin, one of the engineers working on the movie soundtrack, recalls Bob's reaction: "He was absolutely furious, and he started yelling and shouting at her. Someone asked him why he became that terribly upset, but Bob didn't give an answer."

After a while, Bob started to loosen up and feel a little more comfortable with his surroundings and his companions. He even started to show them how to play this strange new music called reggae. "He would show us how the different instrumental parts should feel and he played and gave examples," recalls Bundrick. "At the house in Nockeby I had a room, Bob had one, and Nash had one. It was like a factory of music. You would hear reggae from Bob, ballads from Nash, and rock ballads from me. Then we would huddle together and see what we all had that would fit together."

It was during one of those informal creative sessions that Bundrick recorded a Bob Marley acoustic medley that would remain under wraps for more than two decades. He took his tape recorder to Marley's room, and captured the homesick musician, accompanied only by his own guitar, singing a collection of Wailers' favorites: "Guava Jelly," "This Train," "Cornerstone," "Comma Comma," "Dewdrops," "Stir It Up," "Cry to Me," and "I'm Hurting Inside." The medley—minus "Cry to Me"—was included on the lavish and hugely successful four-CD boxed set *Songs of Freedom*, which was released in 1992.

However, Bob's contribution to the Johnny Nash movie soundtrack was limited to a couple of instrumental tracks. *Want So Much To Believe* was a box-office disaster. It closed less than a week after being released in September 1971 and the soundtrack was shelved.

By then, Bob Marley had been back in Jamaica for several months, and one of the Wailers' dreams had come true. They were back on top of the Jamaican charts, and they were there with a song they'd written, recorded, and produced. Even more important, it had been released on their fledgling Tuff Gong label.

It was a monster, and it rocked Jamaica for much of the second half of 1971. Today, the opening lines are etched into the collective consciousness of millions of Wailers' fans around the planet: "One good thing about music, when it hits you feel no pain."

The song was called "Trench Town Rock."

8.
Introduction to Island

I t's hard to overstate the importance of "Trench Town Rock." Recorded in July 1971, it ruled the Jamaican charts for much of the summer and autumn of that year, spending five solid months at No. 1.

In the years to come it would be the song Bob Marley chose to open many of his most celebrated live performances, and in many ways it was a prototype for the loping, mid-tempo reggae that became Bob's trademark and with which he was to conquer the world without ever compromising his Trench Town roots. In short, it was a monster—and this despite the fact that it was recorded with a highly unconventional Wailers line-up. Missing was the group's new bass player. When Bob had been absent in Sweden, Family Man had taken a temporary job playing calypso on a cruise liner (the mind boggles) sailing between Jamaica, Haiti, and Miami. His bass duties with the group were assumed, with considerable success, by Bunny for the "Trench Town Rock" session and several that followed it before Fams's return in late July. Also on "Trench Town Rock," singing harmony, were Wailers' bredren from their days in Joe Higgs's Trench Town yard— Winston "Pipe" Matthews and Lloyd "Bread" McDonald, from the wonderful roots group Wailing Souls.

The re-energized Wailers were soon turning out single after single on their Tuff Gong label—among them "Screw Face," "Concrete Jungle," and "Guava Jelly," all with Bob on lead vocal, and "Once Bitten," "Lion," and "Here Comes the Sun" (a cover of the Beatles song) featuring Peter on lead.

Glen Adams, the keyboard player from their Scratch days, had by now emigrated to New York, and his replacement for most of the Tuff Gong sessions was a raw teenager who was to play a major role with the Wailers throughout most of the seventies.

Tyrone Downie was just the sort of young talent the Wailers needed. Born in May 1956, he'd joined his school choir, not so much because he wanted to sing but because they had two pianos he could practice on. Singing and playing with the choir had given him a solid foundation in the intricacies of harmony, and while attending Kingston College he'd become friends with another talented young musician, Augustus Pablo. Pablo was already a fixture on the Kingston music scene, and he played regularly with a group called Young Professionals. When they had some engagements he couldn't make, he recommended Tyrone to the group's leader as a replacement.

The leader of Young Professionals was also the Wailers' bass player, Aston "Family Man" Barrett. He was immediately impressed with the precociously talented youngster, and so, at the age of fifteen, Tyrone Downie became a professional musician. To be more accurate, he was playing with a professional band. As well as being a keyboard prodigy, Downie had something else going for him: he was willing to play for free.

Soon the young Downie had become, by his own admission, a Wailers groupie, and was hanging around the group whenever he could, waiting for his big opportunity. It arrived at the outset of their 1971 creative tidal wave. The Wailers were now producing their own music for their own label, and the money for studio time, top-drawer session musicians, pressing, and distribution was coming out of their own pockets. Tuff Gong wasn't making them rich, and Family Man suggested to Bob at a rehearsal that they should give the young keyboard wizard a chance. Tyrone Downie was suddenly a member of the hottest reggae group in Jamaica. And in the best Wailers tradition, he wasn't getting paid for his efforts. "I never used to get any money," Tyrone recalled years later. "I used to get a spliff, some ital juice, you're supposed to just be happy with that."

With Lee Perry by now completely out of the mix, the Wailers also decided to round out their Tuff Gong sound by re-recruiting some of the horn stalwarts from their Studio One era, bringing

Tyrone Downie: Wailers keyboard stalwart in a relaxed mood

Tommy McCook, Vin Gordon, and "Deadly" Headley Bennett back into the studio for many of their 1971 sessions.

Bob Marley's days were full and productive. As well as rehearsing, recording, and playing live shows, he was spending more and more time with Skill Cole, who by now was virtually managing the Wailers. Cole would lead Bob and other members of the Tuff Gong posse in arduous daily training sessions, with a highly competitive game of soccer an unvarying part of their routine. Cole was one of the best players in the world, and Bob was a superbly skilled forward, fiercely competitive, speedy and nimble, and specializing in pin-point passing. Their team was almost unbeatable.

Without question, 1971 was one of the Wailers' vintage years. But they were still primarily musicians not businessmen, and Tuff Gong still wasn't making any money. Being broke was nothing new for Bob, Peter, and Bunny; they'd been that way most of their lives. But that didn't make it any less frustrating, and when Danny Sims told them he wanted them to go to London to do some recording and touring, they decided to take a chance. Sims was hoping to sign the group to CBS in England, and, with Tuff Gong foundering financially, they said yes.

Taking their chances in England was a gamble that paid off in the long run for the Wailers and particularly for Bob Marley, though mostly that first trip was a miserable time for the group. They arrived in London just as winter was setting in, and discovered that Sims and Nash had installed them in a rundown hotel in Bayswater.

The English weather was foul and, to the Wailers, so was the English food. In those days, England was still in the culinary dark ages. It was chips (the English name for French fries) with every-thing—fish and chips; pie, peas, and chips; ham, egg, and chips; sausage and chips . . . one English favorite, known as a "chip buttie," consisted of a heap of greasy chips, heavily salted and doused with malt vinegar, between two pieces of ready-sliced, buttered white bread.

Artistically things weren't much better. Johnny Nash's *I Can See Clearly Now* album, with sanitized reggae versions of four Bob Marley compositions ("Stir It Up," "Guava Jelly," "Comma Comma," and "You Poured Sugar on Me"), was a worldwide smash, by far the biggest of his career, but this was small consola-tion for the group as they languished in their seedy hotel and spent most of their time rehearsing, chasing girls, and looking for food they could stomach.

Bunny, usually the quietest member of the group, was partic-ularly unhappy with the situation—and the success of *I Can See Clearly Now* didn't help matters. To Bunny, Nash was hijacking Jamaican music and getting rich from it while he and his bredren were cold, broke, and hungry in a country he didn't know and didn't particularly care to.

Things improved somewhat when Sims appointed a Londoner of Trinidadian descent, Brent Clarke, to take care of the Wailers.

Clarke quickly moved the unhappy trio—Family Man and Carly had remained in Jamaica—out of their hotel and into a small, semi-detached rented house in the London suburb of Neasden.

The surroundings were nondescript and the weather was still vile, but at least the group had comfortable rooms and a kitchen where they could cook ital food and Bob's beloved fish tea. Bunny was still unhappy and withdrawn, but Bob and Peter, by all accounts, perked up considerably. They soon had local girlfriends and immersed themselves reasonably happily in the lively West Indian runnings in Brixton and Notting Hill, two areas that were home to large numbers of transplanted Jamaicans. The trio even made it into the CBS studio, recording versions of "Stir It Up," "Concrete Jungle," and "Midnight Ravers" around February 1972. None of the tracks were ever released.

Apart from the lively social scene, it was still a frustrating time for the three homesick Wailers. They'd left Jamaica after one of the most intense and productive periods of their career, with their epic "Trench Town Rock" still at the top of the charts, and now they found themselves a long, long way from home and in a state of professional limbo.

Just when it seemed things couldn't get much worse, they did.

Danny Sims and Johnny Nash decided they had to leave for New York to take care of some urgent business. They left England in a hurry, and they left the Wailers in the lurch. They were stranded in London. It was still winter. They had no money, and no prospect of getting any money. A hasty return to Jamaica was clearly in order—but they didn't even have return tickets.

Once again, Brent Clarke came to the rescue. In addition to working occasionally for Danny Sims, Clarke was active in the vibrant Caribbean music scene in London, and one of his contacts was an Anglo-Jamaican who'd had considerable success distributing hot-from-yard singles to the eager West Indian record-buying community. He had then made the switch to mainstream rock, which sold a lot more records and made him a lot more money. His name was Chris Blackwell and his company was called Island Records.

Clarke set up a meeting between the broke and desperate Wailers and the millionaire record company czar. Blackwell had more or less turned his back on Jamaican music for the better part of five years, and when the three Wailers walked into his office in the Basing Street studios of Island Records the odds against them emerging with anything more tangible than words of encouragement seemed prohibitively long.

For one thing, Chris Blackwell was a Harrow-educated, card-carrying member of the Jamaican establishment. His surname came from his Irish father, who was related to the wealthy Blackwell side of the Crosse and Blackwell company, which owed much of its fortune to Britain's collective taste for a mayonnaise-like concoction known as "salad cream," ritually and liberally doused by families throughout the nation on an unimaginative mix of lettuce, tomato, cucumber, and hard-boiled egg—the British concept of healthy eating. His mother was a Lindo, a member of one of Jamaica's richest families.

Although born in England, in 1937, Blackwell was living in Jamaica before he was a year old. His family home wasn't that far from Trench Town, but it might as well have been on another planet. Blackwell spent the first few years of his life in a gracious, sprawling mansion on Waterloo Road, the most prestigious home in Kingston's most prestigious neighborhood. It was called Terra Nova, and it was one of the most magnificent houses in all of Jamaica, with immaculately coiffed grounds, elegant verandas, and an assortment of stately formal rooms and opulent bedrooms.

Blackwell, though, was a lonely child. He was living in almost unimaginable luxury, but he had no one his own age to have fun with. If he'd known they existed, he would probably have envied the kids playing in the streets in the nearby ghetto areas.

The young Blackwell's progress through life, at least in his early years, was preordained. At ten, he was sent back to England so he could get the sort of education wealthy Caribbean families thought was essential for the continuation of their elitist dynasties. At fourteen, he went to Harrow, which ranks alongside Eton as the most exclusive of England's so-called "public" schools—which aren't open to the public and for which prospective pupils have to be registered almost from birth . . . assuming that they're born into a suitably rich and/or aristocratic family. Properly educated, he landed a job with the accounting firm of Price Waterhouse, but he soon found another, infinitely more interesting, occupation that also involved numbers. For several years in his late teens Blackwell made a living gambling, playing games of chance at London's hip nightclubs and betting on greyhound and horse racing.

In his early twenties Blackwell moved back to Jamaica, where his place in colonial society awaited him. He flirted with a number of jobs—including one as aide-de-camp to the British governor — but after just over a year he found the one that suited him best: he got into the music business.

One of Blackwell's jobs had been teaching water skiing at the exclusive Half Moon Bay hotel, not far from Montego Bay on Jamaica's north coast. He'd quickly been captivated by the music of a Bermudian jazz group playing there, led by a talented pianist called Lance Heywood. Intrigued by their commercial possibilities, he had set up his own record company. *Lance Heywood at the Half Moon* was the first album released by Island Records. It was a modest start for a company that Blackwell would sell for more than US$300 million a couple of decades later.

In 1962, with the fledgling Jamaican recording industry clearly on the verge of an explosion, Blackwell decided that he'd be better off back in London, where there was not only a solid core market for Jamaican music but also a lot more potential for eventual expansion. He signed distribution and licensing deals with many of the leading Jamaican producers, and started successfully marketing their records in England, carrying stacks of 45s in his Mini Cooper—the trendies' car of choice in the sixties—to the small record stores that served the West Indian communities that had sprung up all over London in the wake of the massive wave of Caribbean immigration during the previous decade. These stores,

Chris Blackwell, the founder of Island Records. He took a chance with the Wailers, and the gamble paid off.

like Desmond Hip City on Railton Road in Brixton, were popular hangouts in an era when young black Britons were forging an identity for themselves in a country where they were being constantly harassed and often physically abused by racist cops, and they were always eager for music that spoke to them in their own words and encouraged them in their struggle. Business was brisk for Blackwell, and many of these hot new singles were hits, although the young entrepreneur didn't have a great deal of luck with "Judge Not," a 45 on Leslie Kong's Beverley's label by a singer he hadn't heard of called Bob Marley.

In 1964, Blackwell got his big break. And it was huge.

The song was "My Boy Lollipop." It was arranged by the brilliant Ernest Ranglin and recorded in a bouncy near-ska tempo by a virtually unknown young Jamaican singer called Millie Small. Licensed by Blackwell to the giant Phillips label, it sold something like six million copies worldwide, and Blackwell promptly signed a management contract with Millie.

His next big break came almost immediately. He booked his new artist for a tour in support of her No. 1 hit, and one of the gigs was in the Midlands city of Birmingham. Millie, of course, topped the bill wherever she performed in those days, and Blackwell, always on the lookout for new talent, was impressed by one of the opening acts at the Birmingham show. They were called the Spencer Davis Group, and they were led by the keyboard player after whom they were named. But it wasn't Spencer Davis that Blackwell was interested in, it was his lead singer, Stevie Winwood.

Winwood had a penetrating, gravelly blues voice that sounded as though he'd spent thirty years paying his dues on the chitlin' circuit in the southern USA. And he knew how to use it, despite the fact he'd just turned fifteen. As usual, Blackwell moved quickly. He signed the Spencer Davis Group to Island and the following year had another huge hit to his credit. It was called "Keep on Runnin'," and it was followed by another two international smashes, "Gimme Some Lovin'," and "I'm a Man."

Chris Blackwell had moved into the pop mainstream, and before long the mainstream had made him a millionaire—an occupation he'd been born to, after all.

By the time he met the Wailers, Blackwell had more or less cut his ties with Jamaican music. But the meeting with the young Rasta musicians turned Blackwell's thoughts back to the years he'd spent in Jamaica—in particular, he recalled an incident when he'd been out with friends on his motorboat. The boat had hit a reef and been swamped, and they had to swim for shore. They had ended up on an isolated beach, and the tired, hungry, and thirsty Blackwell set off alone in search of help. After some hours, almost overcome with exhaustion, he found it—at a Rasta beach encampment. It was the aristocratic Blackwell's first close encounter with

Rastafarians, and initially he was more than a little apprehensive, wondering what would happen to him next. What happened was that the Rastas fed Blackwell, preached to him earnestly about their religion and Haile Selassie, then took him to Kingston, where he quickly organized the rescue of his stranded friends. The incident changed forever how Blackwell would view an element of Jamaican society that people of his lofty social status had always regarded with a mixture of fear, suspicion, and contempt.

So he was more than willing to listen to what Bob, Peter, and Bunny had to say when they strutted into his Basing Street office—their cockiness and confidence belying the fact that they were broke and desperate. Recalls Blackwell: "The three of them came in, and they were nobodies but they were like huge stars, their attitude and the vibe they gave off. We met and I really just took to them, this attitude they had. It could be conceived to be very aggressive or very negative but I really didn't see it as that. They were like real sort of rebels, they were prepared and they were ready to work but they wanted to do everything pretty well on their own terms. And so I made a deal with them which in a sense was risky, which was to contract with them to give them some money to go off and make a record. Everybody said they'll never make the record and you'll never see the money again, that'll be that, because they had a bad reputation. The amount was four thousand pounds."

For the Wailers, who'd always had huge hassles getting producers to part with a few dollars for songs that were chart smashes, finding a record company boss willing to trust them with thousands of pounds as an advance for music they hadn't even made was a revelation. They were determined not to let Blackwell down, and they didn't. They quickly flew back to Jamaica to record the promised album.

It was called *Catch a Fire*, and although no one knew it at the time, it was going to change the history of popular music.

9.

Catching a Fire

J amaicans make a lot of music, and they make it quickly. In the modern era, the island's prodigious output owes much to technology, and computerized rhythm tracks—a soulless abomination in the eyes of many—now dominate the JA recording scene. In the past, the volume of music emerging from Jamaican studios was equally high, but it was all made by human hand, and it wasn't at all unusual for top session men to spend a full weekend in a studio churning out track after track, pausing only to refuel on food and a spliff, and to catch a quick nap now and again.

So while it would be unheard of in the mainstream pop world, it's not really surprising that *Catch a Fire*, the Wailers' first album for Island Records and one of the landmark recordings in music history, was completed in three epic sessions at Kingston's Dynamic Sound studios in October 1972.

To Bunny Wailer, in fact, it was all quite routine. "As some of the songs that are on *Catch a Fire* were songs that were already recorded by the Wailers, it wasn't any kind of a hassle to do the album, it was simply a Wailers type thing—going into the studio and doing a lot of work. Blackwell was sitting down wondering if we were ever going to return with the album. So it was a challenge for us to prove to him, yunno, different from what he thought. So we just had to get to the point. So the album was done in, like, record time."

Blackwell recalls that, a few months after advancing the group the money to record Catch a Fire, "I went down to Jamaica and I rang them up and I wondered if I was going to hear anything and if there was anything to hear. And they came round and picked me up at my hotel and they played me Catch a Fire. I know enough about recording to know that four thousand pounds was in that record and they'd put every penny in it."

Over the years, there have been many conflicting and wildly varying versions of exactly where and when these historic tracks were laid down. The most authoritative account of who played and on which tracks is contained in the epic and painstakingly compiled Bob Marley and the Wailers: The Definitive Discography, whose authors interviewed many of the musicians, including Bunny Wailer.

First came the riddims.

These were recorded on two consecutive days in early October, and the core members of the Wailers—Bob Marley, Peter Tosh, Bunny Wailer, Aston Barrett, and Carlton Barrett—were augmented by a host of the island's leading session musicians, some of whom were soon to become full-fledged members of the group's ever-changing line-up. Among them were: Robbie Shakespeare (bass); Tyrone Downie (organ); Alvin "Seeco" Patterson (percussion); Earl "Wya" Lindo (piano); Winston Wright (organ); Bernard "Touter" Harvey (keyboards); Ian "Munty" Lewis (bass); Roger Lewis (guitar); Cat Coore (guitar); Alva "Reggie" Lewis (guitar), and Winston "Sparrow" Martin (drums). Interestingly, there wasn't a single horn player in any of the sessions.

Once the riddims were in place, Bob, Bunny, and Peter rehearsed their vocals for a week or two and, astonishingly, recorded them all in a single day. Bob sang lead on "Concrete Jungle," "Slave Driver," "Kinky Reggae," "No More Trouble," "Midnight Ravers," and "Rock It Babe," and Peter took the lead on "400 Years" and "Stop That Train." Bunny sang harmony and played percussion on all the tracks, and took over bass duties on "Rock It Babe," while Rita Marley and Marcia Griffiths contributed harmony vocals on "Rock It Babe."

Two tracks that were recorded during these sessions didn't make the final cut for *Catch a Fire*: the lovely "High Tide or Low Tide" and a somewhat clichéd love song titled "All Day All Night."

Within a few days of the final *Catch a Fire* session, Bob Marley again parted company with his musical comrades in arms. This time, however, he wasn't heading for the United States to visit his mother and try to earn cash for the Wailers—he was on a plane to London, with the precious eight-track master tapes of *Catch a Fire* in his carry-on bags and never out of his sight.

Although he almost certainly didn't know it when his plane was taking off from Norman Manley International Airport, he was about to play a major role in making some radical changes to the music the Wailers had just recorded.

Chris Blackwell wasn't only a brilliant entrepreneur. He had an unerring sense of what people wanted to hear—and not only Jamaican people. Blackwell hadn't fronted the Wailers four thousand pounds because he wanted to sell a few hundred copies of their record to West Indian stores in and around London—his horizons were much, much broader. He was determined to break the group internationally, and his gut instinct told him that the drum-and-bass-driven music they'd recorded in Jamaica was just too heavy for the global market. It might have had a Jamaican audience up and skanking at a sound-system dance in Kingston, but it wasn't going to work the same magic on a hip night club crowd in London's West End or New York's Greenwich Village.

He was determined to make *Catch a Fire* more palatable to reggae neophytes, and he couldn't help wondering what sort of reception his plans to soften the sound of the Wailers would get from Bob Marley. He needn't have worried. Bob may have been unbending when it came to rehearsing and perfecting his music, but he never hesitated to make sensible accommodations he thought would help it to sell—and to carry his message to people throughout the world.

The mixing of *Catch a Fire* didn't take long—the album was released in December, about two months after the initial recording sessions—but the changes that were made at Island's studios in Basing Street were substantial. In effect, they involved toning down the bottom end, bringing the high end forward, and adding some rock-flavored guitar and keyboards. Two top-drawer American studio musicians were enlisted by Chris Blackwell to embellish the Wailers' rootsy sound: a brilliant Texan guitarist, Wayne Perkins, and keyboardist John "Rabbit" Bundrick, who had lived and worked with Bob during his less than happy time in Sweden in 1971. Their memories of the mixing of *Catch a Fire* are illuminating.

Wayne Perkins remembers: "They started playing this strange music, that I've never heard the likes of. Compared with anything else I'd ever heard in my life, the R 'n' B, the church music, this was back to front. So I'm listening and I'm sitting trying to find out what's goin' on and I can't find what, to save my ass I cannot find what. So I'm going, 'Chris, what's going on?' He said, 'Don't listen to the bass' and he brought the bass down for me a little bit and I'm listening and all of a sudden something starts to settle in and so I said, 'All right, roll the tape.'"

The "tape" was "Concrete Jungle," the first track on *Catch a Fire*. And the wailin' guitar that introduced thousands of reggae fans to the music of the Wailers was played by Perkins, as was the memorable solo in the middle of the track. "I had this pedal on at the end of the solo, which was a sustain pedal from Manny's that I'd bought in New York, and you hit this thing and it just like held the note forever. And it held that one note and would start to feed back in an octave higher, and then two octaves higher than that, and when that happened, Blackwell or somebody, maybe Tony [Platt, the remix engineer at Island], hit the echo on that thing and it like rang across the whole room, it even gave me goose bumps. It was one of those magic moments, and then Marley came running out trying to cram a spliff this long down my throat, just jumpin' up and down patting me on the back going, 'That's it, man' and I had no idea what he was saying."

"Rabbit" Bundrick remembers his part this way: "Bob had his guitar on and he was going chick-a chick-a and I was just meandering on the organ and he was saying, 'No, No, NO, bumbaclot, rassclot,' and all this you know and he said, 'The organ, man, the organ go like this.' And he came over to the organ and he didn't play any notes he just slapped the keys and said, 'I go chick-a and you go like that,' and I said, 'Like this?' and he said, 'No, No, NO, play the chord, like me.' And I made it a chord . . . It's what he could teach you about his music that helped you with your own music. Feelings, playing from the heart, things like that."

Blackwell recalls: "This record had the most overdubs on it. This record was the most I don't say softened, I more say enhanced, to try to reach a rock market because this was a first record and they wanted to reach into that market.

"Bob always seemed to have a very clear idea of what he wanted from the recordings. He would record everything, all the tracks, and I would basically mix them and put them together in an arrangement and compile the albums in terms of their running order. Somebody said to him one time was I his producer and he said no I was his translator and I liked that, I was very happy with that. I think that was probably what I was doing.

"Frankly, on hearing *Catch a Fire* now I prefer it in the raw version, it sounds to me much better than what we actually did with it. But at the time one was really trying to change a perception and reach a market."

During the remixing of *Catch a Fire*, Blackwell also came to realize something of considerable significance about Bob Marley's voice and what made it so special. "He has a great voice for recording. It's in the frequencies that you need to cut through the instruments . . . You could surround it with instruments at a high level but his voice is at a frequency that it can cut through."

With *Catch a Fire* by now mixed to the satisfaction of both Bob Marley and Chris Blackwell, there was one more hitch before it could be released: the Wailers were still under contract to Danny Sims.

It could have been a huge problem, so Bob flew to New York, where Sims was busy working on promoting a Johnny Nash reggae-pop version of "Stir It Up," to see what could be done. Sims listened to what Marley had to say, and agreed to sell the Wailers' recording and management contract to Island Records for a fairly modest sum and a small cut of their album sales. The astute Sims also insisted on Bob signing a new songwriting contract with his company, Cayman Records. It was an agreement that was to have legal repercussions many years after Bob's death.

Blackwell wasted no time in agreeing to Sims's terms, and *Catch a Fire*, the first reggae album to be marketed internationally and innovatively packaged (it came in a jacket with a lighter-like flip-top lid), was a resounding success; not in record sales—they were a comparatively modest 14,000 in its first year—but with the all-important music press, who greeted it with rapturous reviews, and with hip club audiences on both sides of the Atlantic.

The Wailers had gone international. They weren't the first Jamaican musicians to make it big outside the island—*The Harder They Come*'s brilliant soundtrack had introduced millions of people around the world to reggae a few months earlier, and Desmond Dekker's "Israelites" had topped international charts three years before *Catch a Fire* was released. But the music of the Wailers was a new and different reggae sound, far heavier despite the extensive remix, and it was creating a different sort of buzz.

Chris Blackwell decided right away that he needed a follow-up album—and that it was time for the Wailers to start touring in support of *Catch a Fire*. For the Wailers, it was a new beginning. And, though they didn't know it, it was the beginning of the end for the original group.

Back in Jamaica, Bob had a new headquarters—and a new love interest. He was now living uptown, in a sprawling colonial mansion that Blackwell had recently purchased and given Bob and his bredren the run of. The house, which Bob was soon to purchase outright from Blackwell, was at 56 Hope Road—an address that was to become just as synonymous with Bob Marley and reggae music as Trench Town itself.

When he wasn't rehearsing, playing soccer with Skill Cole and the rest of the House of Dread team, or visiting Trench Town in search of old friends and fresh herb, Bob was pursuing a torrid affair with a world-famous Jamaican actress, Esther Anderson. Rita had given birth to their third child, Stephen, on 20 April 1972, and had moved from Kingston with Sharon, Cedella, Ziggy, and the new infant to Bull Bay, about ten miles from Kingston, where there was a thriving Rasta enclave. Bob would visit her—and other "baby mothers"—occasionally, but his main romantic interest in

Feel that spirit: Bob on stage, circa 1973

1973 was Anderson. The beautiful actress, who was born in 1945, the same year as Bob, had just starred alongside the Oscar-winning, Bahamian-born actor Sidney Poitier in a movie called The Warm December, but she was equally well known for a well-publicized seven-year relationship with another Oscar-winning actor, Marlon Brando. Her other acting credits included roles in two landmark British television series, Dixon of Dock Green and The Avengers, and in the 1965 movie Genghis Khan, in which she played a concubine.

Anderson, who had been sent by Blackwell to help manage the band, remembers Bob in those days as being down-to-earth, innocent, and unsophisticated in many ways, and astute and worldly in others.

"When I met Bob I was twenty-nine and I loved him very much, I really loved him. I believed in him. I believed in all of them—all of them. They were people who did not have anything to do with the system, yet they knew exactly what was going on with the world outside Jamaica. They listened to the radio, the BBC, or they read the newspapers and they read the Bible, and from that they brought out everything as to their philosophy and what place we were in time.

"Bob didn't believe in too much smiling, because his thing was when you come down to the rock and see how hard life is, then you see why I don't smile. But when he did smile he had such a wonderful smile. Then I found out he had kids. I didn't know during this relationship that he was married and had kids all over the place. I was absolutely flabbergasted—I said how can you, a young boy, have so many children? I didn't know that he had many, many more! He was a country boy, very, very simple, very unso-phisticated. He might have acquired a bit of sophistication later on as he became famous, but when I met him he was totally inno-cent—that's why I thought it was unbelievable that he had children. I thought of him as a little boy."

Esther Anderson had become a big part of Bob's life, but there was something even more important: music. And when the time came to record a second album for Island, the Wailers got down to business with the professional efficiency that was the result of their countless hours of rehearsing and recording over the previous decade.

Burnin' was an eclectic mix. There were three Wailers' favorites from their Coxson Dodd and Lee Perry eras with Bob on lead vocals: "Put It On," "Small Axe," and "Duppy Conqueror," each recorded with a radically different approach from the original. First time around, these tracks had the unmistakable stamp of the strong-willed studio czars who'd been at the controls. On *Burnin'*, they had the unmistakable stamp of the Wailers themselves, with Family Man's thunderous bass and Carly's insistent snare defining a dread-heavy sound that would seduce new fans around the world without compromising the group's Jamaican roots. *Burnin'*'s militancy was underscored by three rebellious new numbers: "I Shot the Sheriff" and "Get Up Stand Up" were a pair of anthemic reggae-rockers that would become staples of Wailers live performances in the years ahead, while "Burnin' and Lootin'" carried a message that was even more immediate and threatening. Bob always insisted this wasn't a song to take literally—"Burning all illusion tonight" were the key words, he maintained—but on the surface, at least, this was the most incendiary number the Wailers had yet recorded. The album wasn't all fire and brimstone: Bob also took lead vocals on "Rasta Man Chant," a glorious anthem to Rastafari, while Bunny was given an all-too-rare opportunity to showcase his still-angelic falsetto on "Hallelujah Time" and "Pass It On," two beautiful and highly spiritual tracks credited to his wife, Jean Watt.

Somewhat ominously, Peter had to settle for a solitary lead vocal spot, on "One Foundation," along with a single verse of "Get Up Stand Up," a song he'd co-written with Bob. The proud Tosh wasn't overjoyed at being relegated, as he saw it, to a supporting role, and the depth of his growing agitation would shortly become apparent.

Soon after the album was completed, the group was on a plane back to London for a brief but hectic tour to promote *Catch a Fire*. They played mostly at colleges and universities in the industrial Midlands and North, along with a few pub gigs in the South—

twenty-eight dates in just over a month, many of them involving two sets a night. It was grueling in every way. The group was touring on a shoestring, traveling in a tiny van and usually setting up and tuning their instruments themselves. No one was having a good time, but Bunny, always the quietest and most introspective, was particularly unhappy. He hated everything about touring, from the gray and damp English weather to the gray and soggy English food—and it didn't help that herb was hard to find.

Somehow the Wailers managed some of their most memorable performances during that miserable month. The highlight of the tour was five consecutive nights at the Speakeasy, a trendy London club favoured by musicians and music biz types, where they mesmerized the hard-to-impress audiences (including a young guitarist called Junior Marvin). The group also made a landmark television appearance on the BBC's *Old Grey Whistle Test*.

But the Wailers couldn't have been happier when the tour was over and they were heading back to Jamaica, where they were assured of sunshine, a plentiful supply of good herb, an abundance of ital food and a warm welcome from their various ladies. They flew to Kingston early in June—and almost as soon as their plane had landed Bunny took his leave of the group and headed for Bull Bay.

He would never tour with the Wailers again.

For all but Bunny, the group's return to Jamaica was to be brief. Blackwell also wanted to break them in the United States, and they had been booked for a hastily arranged tour that was to start in Boston in July. Bunny refused to budge from his decision never to tour again—he didn't leave Jamaica for more than fifteen years—and the Wailers, with their US dates fast approaching, desperately needed someone to fill in for his crucial harmonies and percussion and his inimitable roots vibes.

They turned to their old Trench Town teacher and mentor, Joe Higgs, and asked if he'd join them in the States. Higgs agreed, and early in July 1973 the Wailers flew to Boston, where they'd been booked into a jazz club called Paul's Mall. Once again their schedule was back-breaking: they kicked off the tour with a week of three shows a night in Boston, then, still on a shoestring, they embarked on a dizzying set of dates that took them first to New York for a week at Max's Kansas City in Manhattan, where they opened for an up-and-coming young singer called Bruce Springsteen, then to San Francisco, where they played at a club called the Matrix. "We toured from east to west, north to south," recalled Joe Higgs. "We went to a lot of places that a lot of people have never been to in the reggae circuit."

By August, the Wailers were back in Jamaica. But again, it wasn't for long. They had been booked for another tour of the States, this time to promote *Burnin'*, which was released—again to critical acclaim—in October 1973. Bunny still refused to tour, and Joe Higgs once more agreed to fill in on backing vocals and percussion.

The tour started in October, and it was almost a complete disaster. The Wailers had been booked to open for Sly and the Family Stone, one of the hottest acts in the world at the time. The contrast between the psychedelic flash of Sly and the ultra-casual Wailers, who were accustomed to taking the stage in whatever clothes they happened to be wearing that day, could hardly have been greater.

Sly, who was huge at the time, was far from amused when his supposedly loyal fans showed more than passing interest in the upstart young Rastas. After only a handful of shows, the Wailers were fired—in, of all places, Las Vegas. And, of course, they were penniless. Being broke was hardly a new experience for the group —but being broke and stranded in a city that was the quintessential embodiment of Babylon was about as miserable as it could get. They managed to make their way to San Francisco—how remains something of a mystery—where they had been booked for a live performance on KSAN-FM, a cutting-edge rock station. Somehow, the band summoned enough energy to broadcast a superb concert from the Record Plant in Sausalito. They followed it up with a concert back at the Matrix in San Francisco and then moved on to Los Angeles for their final performance in the States. Joe Higgs, by now almost as disillusioned with touring as the man he'd replaced, caught the first available flight back to Jamaica, and the rest of the group headed north to Canada, where they'd agreed to perform at a late-October Ethiopian famine relief concert in Edmonton, Alberta. They did three numbers—"Slave Driver," "Stop That Train," and "Get Up Stand Up"—for a thoroughly baffled and confused audience, who rewarded their efforts with a smattering of half-hearted applause.

The Wailers' touring experiences in 1973 had been dismal— and they were about to get even worse.

They were barely back in Jamaica than they were due to return to England, towards the end of November, for another hastily arranged and badly organized tour. By this time Joe Higgs had had enough of life on the road and refused to go; five demoralized Wailers—Bob, Peter, Family Man, Carly, and "Wya" Lindo—flew to England after only a week or so of home comforts. The English weather quickly laid Peter low, and the first five shows, in London, had to be cancelled when he came down with an attack of bronchitis.

The tour eventually started on 19 November in Nottingham, and the Wailers spent just over a week playing a total of eleven gigs in some of England's grimmest cities. The bone-numbing cold and damp of places like Liverpool, Doncaster, Stafford, Manchester, Bradford, Leeds, and Northampton were too much for Peter, whose bronchitis returned, and the nightmarish tour was over less than two weeks after it began. It was the last time Peter Tosh would tour as a Wailer. They were to make a handful more stage appearances together in Jamaica, but to all intents and purposes the original Wailers had broken up.

While the group had once been like brothers—"we were one for all and all for one," Bunny reminisced fondly long after they split up—the parting of three such immense talents, whose street-tough personalities had been forged in the unforgiving alleys of Trench Town, was never going to come about without some measure of recrimination and, occasionally, downright hostility.

What happened to the Wailers was not exactly unprecedented at the loftiest levels of popular music when massive talents and matching egos come cascading together, often resulting in sublime music and monumental rows: Mick Jagger and Keith Richard have fallen in and out of love, professionally speaking, more frequently than the average Hollywood spotlight couple, while John Lennon and Paul McCartney—arguably the only songwriting team in music history with a sense of melody on par with Bob's—weren't even on speaking terms for years.

Common wisdom is that Peter left the Wailers because he was angry that Chris Blackwell wanted to make Bob Marley the focal point of the group, and Blackwell himself readily concedes that he probably played a big role in the break-up. However, Bob had been the focal point of the Wailers almost from the beginning, going back to their ska days with Coxson. Many of the singles the group released on Coxson's various labels were credited to "Bob Marley and the Wailers," and so were many of the singles on the group's Wail N Soul M label, on Lee Perry's Upsetter label, and then on the Wailers' own Tuff Gong label.

Whatever the underlying reasons, the departure of Peter was bitter. Soon after leaving the group, the always inventive Tosh took to referring to Chris Blackwell as Chris "Whiteworse"— because "he isn't black and he isn't well"—and he's reputed to have threatened Blackwell with a cutlass during one meeting.

Blackwell wasn't the only target of Peter's acid tongue. He was to make some unpleasant remarks about Bob, even resorting to below-the-belt jibes about his old friend's mixed parentage. In a radio interview in Chicago around 1975, Peter was particularly savage.

"This society don't like the truth, the truth always cause offense. For instance, when I told a journalist that I taught Bob Marley to play music he was offended by that. Because maybe I was too black to teach a white man's son music, seen, so I don't know what's the conflict all about because it's the whole general shitstem of underestimating a black man's integrity, seen, especially when you're fundamental black, and I realize I am too black for the business because my business is truth and rights and if I can tell them a simple truth like that and they're offended, suppose I tell them TRUTH? Music is my business. I taught Bob music and I am proud to say I taught many more musician music cause I taught Bunny Wailer music too, I taught Alton Ellis music and they are proud to tell people that, so why should I be ashamed to say I taught Bob music? And then the system, the shitstem, want it to look like I was Bob's student and that is total defamation of my character, underestimation of my ability."

Peter's exodus from the Wailers was probably inevitable and almost certainly for the best. He was far too gifted and far too ambitious to settle for a supporting role, and after putting out a flurry of successful singles in Jamaica on his own Intel-Diplo label he signed with Columbia Records and made the first album of his solo career. It proved, conclusively, that he was a star in his own right. *Legalize It* was a landmark album in the history of reggae. Its title song, with Tosh's huge baritone insisting that his beloved herb be made legal, instantly became the unofficial anthem of marijuana smokers around the world.

The follow-up album, *Equal Rights*, was an even bigger success, and a year or so later, with his career already on a roll, Tosh had a new and powerful ally in his camp. Charles Comer, who played a huge role in Bob Marley's career in the mid and late seventies, became his main PR man, and Peter was suddenly a media darling, playing to packed houses and rave reviews in Europe and North America and with an international hit single, "(You Gotta) Walk and Don't Look Back," a duet with Mick Jagger.

Peter Tosh had a reputation for being something of a prickly character, with a highly individual view of the world and his place in it, a perspective that came from a combination of his own harsh upbringing, his strong Rasta beliefs, and his understandable conviction that people of African descent had been getting a raw deal for centuries. His brushes with authority were legendary, and often took the form of lengthy and volatile speeches in the middle of concerts in which he denounced the "shitstem," "politrics," and any other manifestation of Babylon that he felt strongly about at that moment.

In April 1978, Peter delivered the most controversial and inflammatory speeches of his career. The occasion was the One Love Concert for Peace in Kingston's National Stadium, and Peter was one of the host of reggae stars lending their support. In the audience, making mandatory appearances, were the two most powerful politicians in Jamaica: Prime Minister Michael Manley and his arch-rival Edward Seaga, along with their most influential ministers and cohorts.

Peter had a captive audience, and he couldn't resist telling them exactly what he thought of the way they were running Jamaica. Tosh unleashed not one, not two, but three verbal broadsides at the stone-faced politicians, lit up a spliff on stage in full view of them and hundreds of police and soldiers, and, almost incidentally, delivered blistering renditions of "400 Years," "Stepping Razor," "Burial," "Equal Rights," "Legalize It," and "Get Up Stand Up" (with Robbie Shakespeare marching back and forth on stage brandishing his guitar like an imaginary machine gun as he churned out thundering bass lines).

Tosh's performance that night had some significant repercussions: he was savagely beaten by police a few months later, and survived only by calling on his defensive martial arts skills and then feigning death; and he so impressed Mick Jagger, who was in the audience, that he was signed for the Rolling Stones' Sticky Fingers label, touring and playing huge stadiums on the same bill as the "world's greatest rock and roll band" and recording three albums, *Bush Doctor*, *Mystic Man*, and *Wanted Dread and Alive*, before his relationship with the Stones had run its course in 1981.

Tosh continued to record and tour with considerable success, until, around 1984, he took what amounted to a lengthy sabbatical from the music business. For three years virtually nothing was heard of Peter, until in 1987 he recorded what was to be his last album: *No Nuclear War*, released early in September of that year.

A frequent visitor to Tosh's home around that time was a Kingston bad man called Dennis "Leppo" Lobban. There have been many conflicting stories about Lobban's relationship with Peter and why he turned up at Tosh's home on the fateful evening of 11 September 1987, accompanied by two other men. The most plausible is that Peter had just returned from a trip to New York for the launch of *No Nuclear War*, and that Lobban assumed he'd brought a substantial amount of money back to Jamaica with him.

In the house for what was planned as a social evening were Tosh's common-law wife, Marlene Brown, Carlton "Santa" Davis, the drummer who had succeeded Sly Dunbar in Peter's Word, Sound and Power band, and two other friends, Wilton "Doc" Brown and Michael Robinson. Two more guests were expected, the popular radio DJ Jeff "Free I" Dixon and Dixon's wife Joy, and when there was a knock at the door Robinson assumed it was them and went to let them in. But it was Lobban and his accomplices, all armed, and they pointed a gun at Robinson as they pushed their way into the house.

They started to demand money, and ordered Peter and his guests to lie on the floor, face down. Then there was another knock at the door. This time it was Jeff and Joy Dixon, who were escorted inside by one of the gunmen and forced to lie down with the others.

By now, Lobban was nearly hysterical and, although Peter tried to reason with him, he suddenly started to fire, almost at random. One bullet grazed Marlene's head and went on to hit Joy Dixon in the mouth. An ugly situation had turned horrific, and worse was to come. Doc Brown was shot and killed instantly. Jeff Dixon was shot and mortally wounded. Then Peter was shot twice in the head. Santa Davis and Michael Robinson were also shot. The gunmen fled, and Marlene Brown, bleeding from her wound, ran out of the house and raised the alarm. Peter was rushed to Kingston's University Hospital, where he was pronounced dead on arrival. He was forty-three.

Almost miraculously, Joy Dixon, Marlene Brown, Santa Davis, and Michael Robinson survived.

Lobban was captured, found guilty of murder, and sentenced to death. But the Jamaican government was to declare an amnesty on executions, and many years later Lobban was still in prison — insisting he had nothing to do with the murders and that the first he'd heard of them was on the radio.

Bunny's departure from the Wailers was comparatively low-key. It was no secret that he hated touring: everything about it was alien to him, from the flying to the food to the weather. The Wailers' new priorities, with Bob the undisputed leader and front man, only served to deepen his conviction that he'd be better off on his own. Without ever formally announcing he was calling it quits, he quietly distanced himself from the group and became more and more involved with his own projects.

As he put it at the time: "Although we are not working together physically, we're sending the same message—Rastafari. So we're together still, and will always be together in that sense. Every man has a testimony and a message, and there's so much inside one that it has to be brought out, or else it can hurt. Ideas that could have been good, dem become stagnant. It wasn't planned, but it worked out that it was all for the good, because now all our material is being exposed. Bob has his album, Peter has his album, and I have my album."

Bunny's first post-Wailers solo venture provided instant and abundant evidence that the "quiet Wailer" knew what was good for him and for reggae music. It was called *Blackheart Man*, and it proved beyond any doubt that Bunny Wailer, as he had now named himself, was a massively talented artist whose genius could never have been confined to the role of backup vocals and very occasional lead singer. *Blackheart Man* launched Bunny's solo career to ecstatic reviews and healthy sales. Unshackled from the constraints of working as a member of a group, Bunny was finally being himself, and he was clearly reveling in his new-found artistic freedom.

Bunny released two more superb roots albums, *Protest* and *Struggle*, followed them with the best-forgotten *Hook Line 'n' Sinker*, and then knocked the reggae world on its collective behind with one of the deadliest dancehall albums of all time.

It was called *Rock and Groove*, and for much of 1981 Jamaica's smoky dancehalls were rocking and grooving to songs like "Ballroom Floor," "Another Dance," "Dance Rock," "Jammins," "Cool Runnings," and "Rootsman Skanking," with Bunny's melodies anchored by the newest crop of studio heavyweights on the Kingston scene: a dreader than dread ensemble called the Roots

Radics that featured Errol "Flabba" Holt on bass, Anthony "Style" Scott on drums, Eric "Bingi Bunny" Lamont and Dwight Pinkney on guitar, and Wycliffe "Steelie" Johnson on keyboards. Bunny was on a reggae roll—a respected pioneer of the music with a command of two of its genres: first roots and now dancehall.

Bunny's subsequent career has been marked by questionable business practices, court battles over royalties—in which he always makes the not unreasonable point that he's entitled to his share of the profits from the music he helped create and record—and a music output that has ranged from fine albums like *Liberation*, *Marketplace*, and *Rule Dance Hall* to less than successful attempts to recapture the dancehall crowd, most of whom have shown little or no interest in an artist their generation regards with the same sort of skepticism the rude boys of the seventies had for the American big band records their parents had danced to.

In concert, though, he remains a majestic and compelling figure, his distinctive tenor—the falsetto of the early years has been consigned to history—clear and penetrating and his onstage persona reflecting the assurance of someone whose path through life has taken many twists and turns, but who knows he's played a crucial role in one of history's great music stories.

For Bob Marley, the departure of Peter and Bunny meant he was the undisputed leader and lead singer of the Wailers. *Catch a Fire* and *Burnin'* had established the group outside Jamaica, and, with Chris Blackwell and Island Records behind him, he could have been forgiven for thinking that he was on the verge of becoming a major international star.

But even Bob, ambitious and determined though he was, couldn't have had an inkling of how huge he was about to become.

10.

Natty Dread

By early 1974, Bob Marley's career was at the crossroads. He had gone international with two albums, *Catch a Fire* and *Burnin'*, he had the backing of a major label, he had a string of hit singles and a decade of experience under his belt in the cutthroat world of Jamaican music, and he'd toured extensively, if not too enjoyably, in England and the United States.

But the departure of Bunny Wailer and Peter Tosh from the Wailers had dramatically changed the dynamic of the group. And there'd been another significant defection: Earl "Wya" Lindo, disillusioned by the chaotic and stressful tours of the previous year, had decided to accept an offer to join the brilliant American-based folk singer Taj Mahal, who had strong Caribbean roots and was in San Francisco.

For a while the Wailers effectively consisted of Bob and the Barrett brothers, with Bob's wife, Rita, as backup singer. Bob had Chris Blackwell in his corner, and he knew that the Island Records boss had enormous faith in him as well as a substantial investment. But he also knew that Blackwell was first and foremost a businessman, and that his business was producing and selling music to a mass market.

It was up to Bob to deliver that music; if he didn't, he could easily find himself back in a government yard in Trench Town, his pockets and his belly empty, and at the mercy, once again, of unscrupulous Jamaican producers.

Jamaica itself was in a state of turmoil. Michael Manley, the charismatic union leader and socialist head of the People's National Party, had won the general election of 1972 by a landslide, and his

The core members of the Wailers throughout most of the seventies: Bob with "Family Man" and Carlton Barrett.

revolutionary economic policies—aimed, essentially, at a dramatic redistribution of the country's wealth—had been vehemently opposed by the Jamaica Labour Party and its conservative leader Edward Seaga, the former proprietor of Federal Studio. Violence was escalating, particularly in the poor areas of Kingston, and the crucial tourism industry was in big trouble as potential visitors read the scary headlines in the foreign press and booked a couple of weeks in peaceful Barbados.

Bob Marley had to act quickly. And he did. He started working on songs for a third Island album, and on rebuilding the decimated Wailers. On his shopping list were two harmony singers, a lead guitarist, and a keyboard player. First came the harmony singers: Marcia Griffiths and Judy Mowatt, who, alongside Rita and known collectively as the I-Three, were to record and tour with Bob for the rest of his career.

Marcia, who had sung harmony on "Stir It Up" during the *Catch a Fire* sessions the previous year, was a solo star in her own right. She'd had an international hit in the early seventies as one half of Bob and Marcia (the other was the superb singer-songwriter Bob Andy) with a reggae version of Nina Simone's "Young, Gifted and Black," one of the anthems of the Black Power movement in the States, and she'd been one of Jamaica's most popular female singers for a decade.

The stunning and deeply spiritual Judy Mowatt had started her career as a dancer, then joined a female trio called the Gaylettes, where her singing brought her to the attention of both Marcia and Rita.

To replace Wya, Bob enlisted the services of Bernard "Touter" Harvey, the young and ambitious keyboard player who had also worked on the *Catch a Fire* sessions and who was in considerable demand in the busy Jamaican recording studios.

Bob also decided to bring horns—missing from both *Catch a Fire* and *Burnin'*—back into the Wailers mix, calling up his old friend from Studio One, Tommy McCook, to play tenor sax, Glen DaCosta, also tenor sax, Vin Gordon, trombone, and David Madden on trumpet. With Seeco on percussion, all that was missing was a lead guitar. That hadn't been a problem with *Burnin'*—Peter had still been with the group, and while he wasn't a flashy lead guitarist, his rootsy "wah wah" sound was more than adequate; reggae, after all, had never had a tradition of showcase guitar solos. But Bob had been impressed with the contributions the Texan Wayne Perkins had made when *Catch a Fire* was being remixed, and he wanted to bring a standout lead guitarist into the Wailers' fold. The only problem being that there was no obvious candidate for the job in Jamaica.

Meanwhile, though, he had an album to make, and early in 1974 the new-look Wailers were back in Harry J's studio in uptown Kingston to start work on the group's third album for Island. This time it was to be an album that established, once and for all, Bob's pre-eminent position in the group.

The album was by "Bob Marley and the Wailers." It was called *Natty Dread*, and it was to be another landmark in the history of popular music, its songs—fervent, angry, revolutionary—establishing Bob Marley as the most powerful protest singer and songwriter the world had ever known and the international voice of Rastafari.

Originally to be called "Knotty Dread"—the change to "Natty," with its very different connotation, was made by Island without consulting Bob—*Natty Dread* was easily the most militant album the Wailers had ever made. It breathed new life into a couple of older Wailers songs: "Bend Down Low" and "Lively Up Yourself." Then there were new, militant compositions like "So Jah Seh" ("not one of my seed shall sit on the sidewalk and beg bread"), "Revolution" ("it takes a revolution to make a solution"), "Them Belly Full" ("them belly full but we hungry; a hungry man is an angry man"), "Talking Blues" ("I feel like bombing a church tonight now that I know the preacher man is lyin'"), and "Rebel Music (3 O'Clock Road Block)" inspired by Bob and Esther Anderson being stopped and harassed by gun-toting police at a road block as they were being driven back to Kingston from their love nest in the beautiful and isolated (in those days) coastal village of Negril.

The band also worked on a song that was to become the most famous on the album and a turning point in Bob Marley's career, although they weren't to record it until they went to London to remix the new album a few weeks after wrapping up the Harry J sessions.

It was called "No Woman No Cry."

The songwriting credits for *Natty Dread* were somewhat misleading—perhaps deliberately so. Bob Marley, who had been "financially disadvantaged," to steal a phrase from Peter Tosh, many times in his career, assigned songwriting credits for many of his best compositions to a variety of friends in order to skirt his contractual obligations to Danny Sims. "No Woman No Cry," the most famous example, was credited to his old Trench Town cohort Vincent "Tata" Ford.

The *Natty Dread* sessions were significant in other ways. They established the female backing trio of Rita, Marcia, and Judy as full-time members of the Wailers, and when Bob, Family Man, and Carly flew to London in August 1974 to mix the album, they were to find the missing link Bob had been looking for to round out *Natty Dread*'s solidly Jamaican riddims—a guitarist who could supply dazzling solos at the lick of a spliff and who was also adept at fitting seamlessly into the ensemble format that was the heart and soul of roots reggae.

It didn't bother the ever-pragmatic Bob in the slightest that he was an American who didn't know the first thing about reggae, about Rastafari, or about Jamaica. Al Anderson could play a mean guitar, and with Bob Marley that was what counted.

Anderson, who had heard only one reggae album in his life — *Catch a Fire*—was a rock guitarist from New Jersey who had an impressive studio track record. He was in London when he was introduced to Chris Blackwell by fellow-guitarist John Martyn, who was signed to Island at the time.

When Bob Marley and the Barrett brothers arrived in London to remix *Natty Dread*, Blackwell thought Anderson could supply the guitar overdubs he and Bob agreed the new album needed, just as Wayne Perkins had with *Catch a Fire*.

At first, Bob, always the perfectionist, wasn't wildly impressed by Anderson's flashy rock solos. But—just as he had with "Rabbit" Bundrick and Wayne Perkins—he persevered, telling the anxious young American he wanted something more bluesy. The versatile Anderson obliged, Bob was happy, and the Wailers had their first full-time lead guitarist. They were to have one until Bob's death, with Al being replaced by Donald Kinsey and Junior Marvin before finally teaming up with Marvin to provide a deadly guitar double whammy from 1978 to 1980. As well as providing the lead guitar overdubs for the *Natty Dread* tracks that had already been recorded in Jamaica, Anderson joined the group in Island's London studios to record "No Woman No Cry."

Bob, Family Man, and Carlton flew back to Jamaica after remixing *Natty Dread*, and were joined there a few weeks later by the group's newest member. It was Al Anderson's first time in Jamaica—and he got an instant introduction to a new way of life.

At first he was frustrated. He'd come to play, and had expected to be recording and touring within days—weeks, at most—of landing in Kingston. Instead, he found himself becoming immersed in the Rasta music runnings in Kingston, at the outset of the golden era of roots reggae. The days became weeks, the weeks became months, and Al Anderson became a familiar part of the Wailers scene, hanging out with and learning from Family Man—as deep and dread a Jamaican as you'll ever find—and the rest of the group, and soaking up the vibes and the reggae that came pounding out of huge speakers in just about every street in the island, a never-ending barrage of drum and bass, roots and culture.

During this comparatively fallow period, Bob Marley got one of the biggest breaks of his life: his first No. 1 international single —at least as a songwriter.

It was also the beginning of a comeback by one of the most revered guitarists in the history of popular music, Eric Clapton.

Clapton, who had become a rock legend with the Yardbirds and Cream in the sixties, and had become even bigger with the monster hit "Layla" with Derek and the Dominos in 1970, had virtually dropped out of sight for three years, battling heroin addiction. He'd finally managed to kick the habit by 1974, and had headed for Miami on vacation. In Miami, the just-recovered and still-fragile Clapton bumped into George Terry, a fellow guitarist he'd met through a mutual friend, Duane Allman, during the recording of "Layla."

Terry was a big fan of a new album called *Burnin'*, by a little-known Jamaican group called the Wailers. Says Terry: "Eric and I wound up hanging out and jamming, and I played *Burnin'* for him during a break." Clapton wasn't impressed—at least not at the beginning. "That was my first taste of Bob Marley, and it took me a while to get into it," he recalls.

But Terry persevered, and eventually the master blues and rock guitarist started to appreciate reggae's riddims and Bob Marley's lyrics. His favorite track was "I Shot the Sheriff," and the recovering Clapton, who had figured it was time he got back to work, decided to include it on his comeback album, to be called *461 Ocean Boulevard.*

Clapton brought together a motley selection of ace studio musicians, and they spent a day rehearsing "I Shot the Sheriff" and trying to master this strange new rhythm. Says Clapton: "It was such a weird melting pot. All I could do to stamp my own personality onto it was to sing it and just play the occasional lick. The rest of it was almost out of control. It was a complete hybrid."

461 Ocean Boulevard was released in July 1974, and the first single taken from it entered the Billboard Hot 100 charts the following month. By early autumn, it had climbed to No. 1. The song was "I Shot the Sheriff," and Bob Marley had his first No. 1 single as a songwriter.

Clapton and Marley had never met, but the guitar legend did get a phone call from Bob while the song was climbing the charts. "We had a half-hour conversation, half of which I understood and half of which I didn't," recalls Clapton.

Understandably, Clapton wanted to see the country that had given birth to reggae music and to the song that had kicked his comeback into overdrive, and by September 1974 the guitarist and his band, including George Terry, were in Jamaica, recording a follow-up album, *There's One in Every Crowd,* at Dynamic Sounds. Clapton had also hoped to meet Bob, but this was Jamaica, and although Bob was on the island he was nowhere to be found.

Clapton wasn't to meet Bob Marley in person until about four years later. The Wailers, by now huge, were touring England, and Clapton went to see their show at the venerable Hammersmith Odeon. "I walked into this dressing room and I couldn't see the other side of it for the smoke," he recalls. "I sat and talked with

Bob, and he was just a *great* guy. He was so warm. A beautiful man. He was serious about what he was doing but he was very gentle. That was our face-to-face meeting."

Things were starting to happen for Bob Marley, and they were happening fast.

He'd gone from being a star in Jamaica to becoming a well-known, if not yet household, name around the world. He was starting to make some real money for the first time in his life. He was the unchallenged leader of the Wailers. And he was as active as he'd ever been when it came to romance.

It's no secret that Bob had numerous affairs, and numerous children—eleven of them acknowledged heirs to his estate, four of them with Rita, seven with other women. There are almost certainly more of whom little is known. Some relatives estimate that he fathered at least twenty-two.

By his own admission, "plenty women" were his main weakness in life, and his numerous liaisons have been written about so often and in so much detail that some people have an image of Bob as a sort of rampant Caribbean Don Juan, ready to bed any attractive female he met.

Before listing his known children briefly, it should perhaps be pointed out that Bob's womanizing has seldom, if ever, been put into a rational cultural context. By the standards of Jamaica and the rest of the Caribbean, Bob Marley's myriad affairs and numerous offspring were no more than routine—certainly nothing to provoke as much as a raised eyebrow. The Caribbean is an earthy, sensual part of the world, and it's not at all unusual for a man to father ten children, fifteen children, or more, by a variety of different women. A classic example is Bob's great bass player, Family Man Barrett, who is reputed to have fathered fifty-two children—and who had another on the way as he celebrated his sixtieth birthday. Similarly, it's equally unremarkable for a woman to have numerous children by a variety of different men.

This was the cultural climate in which Bob Marley was raised, and the fact that he was drop-dead handsome, uniquely charismatic, and disarmingly charming didn't stop women falling for him and falling into his arms. And that was before he became a wealthy, globe-trotting superstar.

He welcomed many of them, had babies with many of them, and never made a serious attempt to hide his affairs—from his fans, from his "baby mothers," or from his wife.

For the record, among Bob Marley's known children are:

Imani Carole (not one of Bob's acknowledged heirs), born 22 May 1963, to Cheryl Murray

Cedella, born 23 August 1967, to Rita Marley

David "Ziggy," born 17 October 1968, to Rita Marley

Stephen, born 20 April 1972, to Rita Marley

Robert "Robbie," born 16 May 1972, to Pat Williams (sometimes known as Lucille)

Rohan, born 19 May 1972, to Janet Hunt (or Dunn, sources vary)

Karen, born 1973, to Janet Bowen

Stephanie, born 17 August 1974, to Rita Marley

Julian, born 4 June 1975, to Lucy Pounder

Ky-Mani, born 26 February 1976, to Anita Belnavis

Damian, born 21 July 1978, to Cindy Breakspeare

Makeda Jahnesta, born 30 May 1981, the month Bob died, to Yvette Crichton

A new generation of Melody Makers: Ziggy Marley (left) relaxes with brother Stephen and sisters Sharon and Cedella at home in Kingston

Bob also adopted and regarded as his own child Sharon Marley, Rita's daughter, who was born in November 1964, before Rita and Bob met.

As much as Bob loved "plenty women," music always came first, and when *Natty Dread* was released by Island Records early in 1975, with Eric Clapton's version of "I Shot the Sheriff" still hugely popular around the world, it was enormously successful, selling well and getting even more ecstatic reviews than *Catch a Fire* and *Burnin'.* The Wailers were on something of a roll, and it clearly was time to think about touring again. The group hadn't been on the road since their horrendous experiences in 1973, and one of Bob's big concerns was that they didn't have a manager. Chris Blackwell had played a major role in producing, remixing, and marketing their music, but he wasn't about to get involved in the nitty-gritty of arranging concert dates, booking hotel and motel rooms, making sure the band and the instruments all made it to the airport and the team bus on time, and ensuring there was a plentiful supply of herb available at all times.

Without a full-time, reliable manager, Bob was reluctant to commit the group to another tour, but he did agree to a rare performance in Jamaica, where the Wailers hadn't played for almost two years.

He even persuaded Peter Tosh and Bunny Wailer, by now concentrating on their own solo careers, to rejoin the group to open for the legendary Motown singer Marvin Gaye, who was headlining a charity concert at the Carib Theatre in Kingston. The show was an instant sell-out. Gaye was a huge attraction worldwide, and Jamaicans were equally keen to see their Wailers perform live after such a prolonged absence.

The show was a sensation. The Jamaican audience—which included a beautiful young girl from uptown Kingston called Cindy Breakspeare—loved the new songs and the new sound of the Wailers, with Bob, Bunny, and Peter swapping lead and background vocals and three stunning Rasta princesses, Judy, Rita, and Marcia, adding their own soaring, soulful harmonies.

They opened with "Curfew (Burnin' and Lootin')" and "Slave Driver" with Bob, by now an even more riveting stage performer, on lead. Peter took over with "Can't Blame the Youth," Bunny followed with "Arab Oil Weapon," and then it was time for "Get Up Stand Up" and finally "Road Block," a song that any Jamaican who's been stopped in a road block—which meant, de facto, just about any Jamaican—could identify with.

Once the Wailers were finally allowed to yield the stage to Marvin Gaye and his thirty-piece orchestra, who were something of an anticlimax after the local "opening act," they were hanging backstage with spliffs and bredren when Bob was approached by Gaye's road manager, a jive-talking man with the sort of in-your-face cockiness and self-assurance that would normally have made the laid-back Rasta shy away.

His name was Don Taylor, and he told Bob he wanted to be the Wailers' manager. A Jamaican who'd spent much of his life in the United States, Taylor looked and sounded like a straight-out-of-central-casting con man, and, as Bob Marley would find out years later, in many ways that's exactly what he was. He was also a shrewd, energetic hustler, with a wide range of contacts in the music business and the sort of energy and let's-get-things-done-now approach that Bob was looking for.

Bob told Taylor he'd think about it.

The following morning, Taylor found his way to 56 Hope Road and made another pitch. Bob, impressed by this distinctly un-Jamaican hustle, said OK, he'd give Taylor a try. It didn't hurt that the move had Chris Blackwell's blessing. He recalls: "Taylor was able to get Bob on the road and bring to life what wouldn't have happened if Bob had not toured. Don Taylor came in and hustled it together. In that respect he was a key man in Bob's success. It wouldn't have happened if Bob hadn't gone out touring, and Don got that together for him."

The Wailers had a new manager. Their CV included three internationally acclaimed albums. They had the backing and support of a label that was both pioneering and major-league mainstream. There was a palpable buzz about their music, particularly among young rock fans who'd grown weary of the glitter-pop of the early seventies. They were ready for the big-time. But they still had no idea how close it was . . . and how big it was going to be.

Mr. Showbiz: Charles Comer, Bob's publicist during the mid to late seventies, in the Reggae Archives in Los Angeles in January 1999, a few days before his death. Comer is pointing to a 1996 picture of himself with Roger Steffens and Bob's son Julian Marley, also taken at the Archives.

11.

The King of Reggae

One of Don Taylor's first jobs for the Wailers was to arrange a major tour, mainly of North America but with a handful of key UK dates, in support of the *Natty Dread* album. Finding suitable venues was no problem for the Wailers' energetic new manager—concert promoters were by now eager to sign the sensational young reggae performer, who was clearly on a fast track to fame and fortune. More importantly to Bob, he was about to have a platform from which he could spread his message of universal love and righteousness to every corner of the earth.

He was also about to become the biggest media sensation since the Beatles ten years earlier. Oddly enough, the man who would stage manage a media blitz that would have Bob's name and face everywhere from mainstream newspapers and magazines to the then avant garde *Rolling Stone*, had also worked with the Beatles when the Fab Four were tearing up the charts on both sides of the Atlantic. His name was Charles B. Comer, and by the time Chris Blackwell hired him to work full-time on making Bob Marley a household name throughout the world, he was already a behind-the-scenes showbiz legend. Comer was from Liverpool, the same tough northern England port city as the Beatles, and it showed. He was a warm, generous, and often sentimental man, with a passion for Nat King Cole ballads and simple, old-fashioned English cooking. He also had a hair-trigger temper, a sometimes venomous tongue, and, if crossed even slightly, would unleash a torrent of rapid-fire abuse, laced with profanity, at whomever had made the mistake of offending him. If the offense was more than slight—or, heaven forbid, if he suspected someone of treating one of his acts less than fairly—he wouldn't hesitate to attack them physically. In his prime, he was a formidable presence, and any overly officious backstage security man who made the mistake of confronting or challenging him would risk finding himself pinned by the throat against the nearest wall and told to get the f**k out of the way. Or else.

"Backstage is mine" was one of Comer's favorite expressions, and he meant it, whether backstage was at Madison Square Garden, Maple Leaf Gardens, the Hollywood Bowl, or Wembley Arena. He also knew just about every entertainment editor and rock writer from Montreal to Melbourne, from New York to London, and was universally feared for his guerrilla phone tactics. His technique was simple: he'd call a journalist anywhere in the world—his phone bills were astronomical—and talk, non-stop, for as long as it took to get a commitment to either review or assign a feature story on one of his clients who happened to be scheduled to perform in their city or town. And it didn't hurt that he'd work only with acts he liked personally and who were worth writing about—among them the Beatles, the Rolling Stones, the Bee Gees, the Who, the Chieftains, Stevie Ray Vaughan, Grace Jones, "Lord of the Dance" Michael Flatley, Marianne Faithfull, Peter Tosh, and, of course, Bob Marley.

Comer's work with Marley and Tosh has seldom been fully acknowledged, largely because he was as adept at keeping himself out of the spotlight as he was at keeping his acts in it. But it's safe to say that while Peter Tosh was a musical giant and Bob Marley a musical genius, without Charles Comer working feverishly to bring them to the attention of newspaper and magazine readers and television audiences throughout the world, neither would have achieved the degree of international fame they did.

Comer joined the Marley media team in the mid-seventies, working out of Island's New York offices, and by the time Bob embarked on his major 1975 tour, soon after the Wailers' Carib Theatre appearance opening for and blowing away Marvin Gaye, it was difficult to pick up a newspaper or magazine on either side of the Atlantic without reading something—be it a snippet in a

gossip column or a major feature—about the man they were calling the King of Reggae. Working in tandem with Island PR
stalwarts Rob Partridge and Jeff Walker, Comer's media campaign
resulted in stories and features on Bob Marley in hundreds of influential publications, among them *Rolling Stone, Melody Maker,* the
Village Voice, even the stately *New York Times*—whose then pop
music critic, Jon Pareles, was one of the first mainstream writers to
recognize Bob's brilliance.

The Wailers' 1975 *Natty Dread* tour started in the United
States, but there was little similarity with the group's disorganized
and stressful experiences of 1973. This time the Wailers didn't have
to carry their own instruments, didn't have to stay in seedy motels,
didn't even have to worry about finding food they could eat. They
had their own cook on the road with them, Mikey Dan, and after
each show the group headed back to their hotel, where Mikey
would soon have a pot boiling with whatever ground provisions he
could find in local stores and markets—yam, sweet potato, eddo,
dasheen, tannia, cassava—along with a cauldron of rice and red
beans . . . and, of course, Bob's favorite fish tea. Spliffs would be
fired up, and the group would flirt and perhaps pair off with
whichever attractive groupies had found their way back to the hotel
with them.

By now the Wailers even had their own art director on the road
with them. Neville Garrick, a brilliant young Jamaican artist, had
joined the Wailers family and was in charge of stage sets—he
created the Haile Selassie backdrop that Bob was to use for just
about every show throughout the rest of his career—and designing
album covers. He was also an enthusiastic and skilled soccer player
and a devout follower of Rastafari, both of which, in Bob's book,
counted for every bit as much as his prestigious UCLA degree.

The *Natty Dread* tour started with a Miami date that served
mainly as a rehearsal, then the Wailers flew north, first to Toronto,
Canada, where they performed at that city's venerable Massey Hall,
and then to Chicago, Detroit, Cleveland, Philadelphia, New York,
and Boston, where they did a week of two shows a night at Paul's
Mall. For Bob Marley, the tour was an endless round of concerts,

Neville Garrick, the Wailers' art director, at work in his Kingston studio in 1988. In the background is the artwork from Bob Marley's posthumous Confrontation *album.*

interviews, and sound checks. And with Don Taylor there to make sure the bus left on time—Bob, as usual the strictest of disciplinarians, was always first on it—he could concentrate on his real mission: getting his message across, both on stage and in interviews. After touring the States and Canada to rave reviews and ecstatic audience reaction, the Wailers crossed the Atlantic for a swift mini-tour in England. There were to be only four performances—one in Birmingham, one in Manchester, and two in London's historic and ornate Lyceum Ballroom on the Strand, where the up-and-coming Jamaican group Third World, who had also been signed by Island Records, were booked as the opening act. The Lyceum shows were to be recorded for the Wailers' first "live" album . . . and they were to result in Bob Marley's first international chart hit.

The dates were 17 and 18 July 1975, and tickets cost only £1.50. Such was the buzz about Bob Marley that both shows sold out instantly, and the police had to be called in to control thousands who didn't have tickets. (Jamaicans, as anyone who's promoted a reggae concert can attest, are notoriously reluctant to part with cash for advance tickets for a concert and equally loath to be told they can't get into a venue when they turn up a few seconds before showtime and discover it's sold-out.)

Both concerts started with the Wailers' favorite show-opener, the incendiary "Trench Town Rock," with the 18 July performance quickly segueing into "Slave Driver," "Burnin' and Lootin'," "Concrete Jungle," "Kinky Reggae," "Midnight Ravers," and "Lively Up Yourself."

Up to that point it was something of a routine Wailers show —tight, professional, visually exciting, but nothing to stamp it as historic.

The next number started with a majestic, soaring organ intro from Tyrone Downie, accompanied by Family Man's massive bass, Carly's insistent drums, and angelic harmony vocals from Rita and Judy (Marcia missed this tour). Al Anderson's exquisite guitar licks were almost overwhelmed in the gospel-like build-up. After a minute, Bob, who had been standing virtually motionless, started to sing: "No woman no cry, no woman no cry; no woman no cry, no woman no cry . . . said, said, said I remember, when we used to sit, in a government yard in Trench Town . . ." It was an electrifying moment.

The studio version of "No Woman No Cry" had been an excellent track on an excellent album, but in the exalted company of numbers like "Them Belly Full" and "Revolution" it hadn't exactly been a standout. The slower, almost hymn-like live version at the Lyceum was something else again. The audience—many of them Jamaican—were transported to another place. They were in that government yard, they could almost smell Georgie's logwood fire and taste the cornmeal porridge, they remembered the good friends they'd lost and they knew, without a doubt, that every little thing was going to be all right.

Bob Marley, in the space of a few minutes, had taken his music and the message it carried to another level.

Bob Marley and the Wailers' Live! was released by Island in November 1975. The show-stopper at the Lyceum had been "No Woman No Cry," and it became Bob's first single in the UK Top 40.

The rest of that live album wasn't particularly memorable. Years later, asked about the Lyceum recording of "No Woman No Cry," Family Man would have this to say: "It was good, like a semi-chant with a little ballad feel. And when we play it we see the response from the audience. On the first live album it seemed to be the only music that seemed to be mixed to the standard of the time. The rest of it sound too tinny, like live stuff."

That first live album may have been flawed, but with "No Woman No Cry" Bob Marley had made another major career leap. In New York, Charles Comer was capitalizing on the single's chart success by orchestrating a media feeding frenzy no reggae artist had even dreamed about in the past. On the strength of a minor chart hit and with the help of the tireless Liverpudlian PR genius, Bob Marley had gone, in the space of a couple of years, from being a star in the Caribbean to a global superstar.

Bob returned to Jamaica in late August to start work on what would be his fourth studio album for Island Records, *Rastaman Vibration*. Al Anderson was about to leave the Wailers—he would return in 1978—to join Peter Tosh, whose solo career was in the ascendancy, and he was replaced on lead guitar for most of the *Rastaman Vibration* sessions by Donald Kinsey, another superb American guitarist with a strong blues background. Taking care of the roots guitar riddims was Earl "Chinna" Smith, a talented young Jamaican much in demand on the frantically busy Kingston studio scene, who was known as the "high priest of the reggae guitar." Once again, Bob Marley had attracted superior musicians to work with him.

With Tommy McCook also back in the line-up, the Wailers returned to Harry J's for another epic recording session. It resulted in a remarkable roster of truly great songs that were to be the core of *Rastaman Vibration*: "Positive Vibration," "Roots Rock Reggae," "Johnny Was," "Cry to Me," "Want More," "Who the Cap Fit," and "Night Shift," the song that had been inspired by Bob's unhappy experiences working at a Chrysler factory in Delaware seven years earlier.

Once again, there was considerable confusion over who'd written which songs. A classic example was "Night Shift." The original

1970 version, "It's Alright," had been released on the Upsetter label and credited to Bob Marley and Lee Perry. The 1975 version, with the same words and the same melody, was credited to Family Man and Carlton Barrett—neither of whom, to the best of anyone's knowledge, had ever driven a fork lift on a night shift. All very inconclusive—which was the object of the exercise.

Then, on 28 August, members of Jamaica's Rastafarian community—and Rastas around the world—were shaken to their collective core by a state media report out of Ethiopia. It said that Haile Selassie I, the man they worshipped as a living god, had died on 27 August from complications following an operation for prostate cancer. After reigning in Ethiopia since 1930, Selassie had been overthrown by the Ethiopian army in September 1974, and placed under house arrest in Addis Ababa. Most of the Imperial family were also imprisoned in Addis Ababa's central prison, known, ominously, as "Alem Begagn"—roughly translated as "I am finished with the world." The emperor's doctor, Professor Asrat Woldeyes, quickly denied that complications from an operation had resulted in Selassie's death, and some believe he was suffocated in his sleep.

Bob never wavered in his belief that the reports were false—he'd often maintained that the man he revered as earth's rightful ruler could, when he wanted, be a baby, or a bird . . . or anything else he chose. So how, Bob reasoned, could such a man die? For Bob Marley, there was only one thing he could do: write a song proclaiming that almighty Jah could never be subjected to the same rules of mortality as ordinary humans. He got in touch with Lee Perry—they'd long since patched up their differences—and they quickly arranged studio time at Harry J's. With Perry once again at the controls, the result was stunning. The song was called, simply, "Jah Live," and in it Bob poured scorn— "fools say in their heart, Rasta your god is dead"—on those who claimed otherwise.

Released as a single on the Tuff Gong label within a few days of Selassie's reported death, "Jah Live" brought much-needed solace to Jamaica's Rastafarians, many of whom had been deeply disturbed by the news out of Ethiopia, and reinforced Bob Marley's growing reputation as the voice of Rastafari.

A few weeks later Bob returned to the studio, this time Joe Gibbs, to record what was to be another landmark tune for the *Rastaman Vibration* album. Titled simply "War," the words are taken almost verbatim from a speech on racial inequality that Haile Selassie—an orator of immense power—had delivered to the General Assembly of the United Nations on 6 October 1963.

With the help of Skill Cole, Bob encapsulated Selassie's speech brilliantly:

Until the philosophy which hold one race
Superior, and another, inferior
Is finally, and permanently, discredited, and abandoned
Everywhere is war, me say war

That until there are no longer, first class
And second class citizens of any nation
Until the color of a man's skin
Is of no more significance than the color of his eyes
Me say war

That until the basic human rights are equally
Guaranteed to all, without regard to race
Dis a war
That until that day
The dream of lasting peace, world citizenship
Rule of international morality
Will remain in but a fleeting illusion
To be pursued, but never attained
Now everywhere is war, war

And until the ignoble and unhappy regimes
That hold our brothers in Angola, in Mozambique, South Africa
In sub-human bondage
Have been toppled, utterly destroyed
Well, everywhere is war, me say war

War in the east, war in the west
War up north, war down south
War, war, rumors of war
And until that day, the African continent
Will not know peace, we Africans will fight
We find it necessary and we know we shall win
As we are confident in the victory

Of good over evil, good over evil yeah, good over evil
Good over evil, good over evil, good over evil

For recording purposes, Bob could hardly have copied the speech in its entirety. But a book has no such constraints, and Selassie's speech on that October day in 1963 was so powerful it deserves a longer excerpt:

Were a real and effective disarmament achieved and the funds now spent in the arms race devoted to the improvement of man's state; were we to concentrate only on the peaceful use of nuclear knowledge, how vastly and in how short a time might we change the condition of mankind. This should be our goal. In saying this we are certain that it is the prayer of humanity.

When we talk of the equality of man we find, also, a challenge and an opportunity to bring men closer to freedom and true equality and, thus, closer to a love of peace.

The goal of the equality of man which we seek is the very antithesis of the exploitation of one people by another, of which the pages of history, in particular those written of the African and Asian continents, speak at such length.

Exploitation thus viewed has many faces. But whatever guise it assumes, this evil is to be shunned where it does not exist and crushed where it does. It is the sacred duty of this organization to ensure that the dream of equality is finally realized for all men to whom it is still denied and to guarantee that exploitation does not reappear in other forms in other places whence it has already been banished.

As a free Africa has emerged during the past decade, a fresh attack has been launched against exploitation wherever it still exists. And in the interaction so common to history, this, in turn, has stimulated and encouraged the remaining dependent peoples to renewed efforts to throw off the yoke which has oppressed them and to claim as their birthright the twin ideals of liberty and equality. This very struggle is a struggle to establish peace, and until victory is assured, that brotherhood and understanding which nourish and give life to peace can be but partial and incomplete.

On the question of racial discrimination, the Addis Ababa Conference taught to those who will learn, this further lesson: that until the philosophy which holds one race superior and another inferior is permanently discredited and abandoned; that until there are no longer any first-class and second-class citizens of any nation; that until the basic human rights are equally guaranteed to all, without regard to race; until that day, the dream of lasting peace and world citizenship and the rule of international morality will remain but a fleeting illusion, to be pursued but never attained. And also, that until the ignoble and unhappy regimes that hold our brothers in Angola, in Mozambique, and in South Africa in subhuman bondage have been toppled and destroyed; until bigotry and prejudice and malicious and inhuman self-interest have been replaced by understanding, tolerance, and goodwill, until all Africans stand and speak as free beings, equal in the eyes of all men as they are in Heaven—until that day, the African continent will never know peace.

We Africans will fight, if necessary, and we know that we shall win, as we are confident in the victory of good over evil.

After recording "War" at Joe Gibbs's studio, the Wailers returned to Harry J's later in September to complete the *Rastaman Vibra-*

Bob at a Kingston concert sound check. Rear, from left, are Neville Garrick, Bunny Wailer, Lee "Scratch" Perry and Alan "Skill" Cole.

tion album with "Rat Race" and "Crazy Baldhead" (the song the then world heavyweight boxing champion Lennox Lewis, a huge Marley fan, played in June 2002, as he entered the ring for a title fight against the shaven-headed Mike Tyson—perhaps unaware that Tyson, too, loved Bob's music; further proof, if any were needed, that Bob Marley's sphere of influence was virtually open-ended).

With the *Rastaman Vibration* tracks in the can, Bob set about rehearsing the Wailers for a tour of North America that the busy Don Taylor had organized for spring 1976. Before that there were a couple of important live shows on the Wailers' agenda, both at Kingston's National Stadium. For the first of them, in September, the Wailers were the opening act for a hot young Motown group, the Jackson Five. Peter and Bunny agreed to rejoin the group for the occasion, but it wasn't a particularly memorable concert.

The following month the Wailers returned to the National Stadium for a show that was considerably more successful—hardly surprising, since the concert was a benefit for the Jamaica Institute for the Blind and the headliner was Stevie Wonder. Bob, naturally enough, was a huge Stevie Wonder fan. And Stevie Wonder, naturally enough, was a huge Bob Marley fan. With Peter and Bunny again agreeing to join the line-up, it promised to be an evening of musical nirvana. It was that, and more.

The Wailers took the stage in the early hours with "Rasta Man Chant," segueing quickly into a nostalgic tribute to their early Studio One days with "Nice Time," "Simmer Down," and "One Love." Then Bunny took the lead with the gorgeous, pastoral "Dreamland," followed by the militant "Battering Down Sentence." Peter was next, with "Mark of the Beast," "Can't Blame the Youth," and his ganja anthem "Legalize It." Bob followed with "So Jah Seh," "No Woman No Cry," and "Jah Live." Then came the most magical moments of the evening, with Stevie Wonder, the greatest soul artist in the world, settling in at the keyboards to jam with Bob on "Superstition" and "I Shot the Sheriff."

Bob Marley, Peter Tosh, and Bunny Wailer, who had started their careers bonded by a love of music and a deep friendship in Trench Town more than a decade earlier, were never to appear on stage together again. There could hardly have been a more fitting final chapter to the story of the original Wailers.   ·

For Bob, the next few years were to bring undreamed of fame, fortune, and adulation. They'd also bring a narrow escape from a violent death—and an injury playing his beloved soccer that was to result in the discovery of a disease from which there was to be no escape.

12.
Ambush in the Night

With the *Rastaman Vibration* sessions and his final live show with Peter and Bunny behind him, and his upcoming tour of the United States months away, Bob Marley was to spend the next few months in Jamaica. It was to be one of his last extended stays in the land of his birth, and, had he known what the future had in store, he'd probably have spent it playing soccer, writing songs, adding to his impressive quota of children, and tracking down the best ganja he could find—all pursuits he engaged in with enormous energy and considerable success.

In New York, Charles B. Comer was applying his enormous energy to sending a virtually non-stop parade of journalists, from a dizzying array of publications, to Jamaica to interview Bob and write stories and features about the charismatic King of Reggae.

Bob, who wanted nothing more than to have his message of Rastafari and universal brotherhood carried to the far corners of the earth, took the arduous interviewing seriously, and for a while 56 Hope Road was transformed into something akin to a global press conference, with Marley assuming the role of a savvy media manipulator, cleverly stickhandling his way around the often intrusive and ignorant questions of some of the interviewers and, without their quite realizing how he'd managed it, contriving to provide them with answers to the questions he thought they really should have asked. Not questions about how many kids he had, why he grew his hair the way he did, why he smoked ganja from morning to night, why he and his bredren believed in the divinity of a man most of them had barely heard of. They didn't know it at the time, but the unassuming, casual, slow-talking Rasta from Nine Mile by way of Trench Town was a whole lot smarter than the big-city journalists who were interrogating him.

One particularly abrasive interviewer asked Bob, sneeringly, "What would I have to do to become a Rastafarian?" Marley visibly recoiled for a fraction of a second—presumably doing a lightning count to ten—and fixed the interviewer with the sort of look that would have had any sane Jamaican stammering an apology and heading for the exit. "You must born again," he snorted, in the tone he reserved for those he found particularly distasteful.

Released in May 1976, *Rastaman Vibration* was the first Marley album to receive less than ecstatic reviews from the press— entirely predictably, given their long and not particularly commendable tradition of building up and knocking down. The fan response was entirely different, however, and the album was soon in both the British and American charts. Compared with the number of Marley albums sold since his death, *Rastaman Vibration*'s figures were modest, but it was the biggest seller Bob was to have in America in his lifetime, and it reinforced his status as a pop music superstar.

The success of *Rastaman Vibration* was hugely important, but before the year was out Bob was to receive an accolade that no one with even a marginal grasp on sanity could have forecast for a reggae musician a year or two previously: *Rolling Stone* magazine, in those days the arbiter of what was hot in the world of pop music, named Bob Marley and the Wailers as the band of the year.

A reggae band had made the cover of the *Rolling Stone*. A dread-locked, ganja-smoking Rasta poet-philosopher-prophet, a country-cum-ghetto youth, who had been living rough in Trench Town at the beginning of the decade, was at the pinnacle of popular culture.

Bob was getting his message across, and the whole world was taking notice.

Along the way, he was also becoming a wealthy man. Not super-rich—not yet, anyway—but his record sales were brisk, his concerts were sell-outs, and he was counting cash in the hundreds of thousands of dollars, with millions clearly on the horizon. And despite having been virtually penniless for just about all of his life, Bob Marley knew exactly what to do with his new-found, undreamed of, wealth.

He started to give it away.

Before long, 56 Hope Road was being besieged by struggling Jamaicans, ghetto people who desperately needed money to feed and clothe their families and themselves. Hundreds would line up, waiting for an audience with Bob. When it was their turn, they'd tell him their story, tell him what they needed and—almost inevitably—they'd get what they asked for. Cindy Breakspeare, by then the main love interest in Bob's life, later estimated that he was supporting something like four thousand people in Jamaica, a figure confirmed by Chris Blackwell. Colin Leslie, who took care of the day-to-day financial runnings at 56 Hope Road for several years when Bob was earning serious money, disagrees. "The figure was much higher than that," he says. "Whenever Bob was in Jamaica, the yard would be filled up with people. It would be over-flowing into the streets, down the sidewalks. We would go into the late hours of the night. He would literally have people lined up and he would be interviewing them, finding out what were their particular needs . . . And he would send them to me and say, 'Give them X amount of money.' And I would write the checks. This would go on until 9, 10, 11, 12 at night, and I would just be writing checks to give these people."

And, just in case any of Bob's people were really hungry, there was always an abundance of food on hand.

Bob Marley always maintained that money meant nothing to him, except that it allowed him to help people. Decades after he left us, a huge reggae hit, one of the few outside the woefully repetitive and negative dancehall genre, had as its chief refrain "by his deeds shall a man be known." Bob Marley would have loved its melody and its message . . . and he'd have been far too modest to realize it could have been written for him.

Jamaica, meanwhile, was once again in a state of turmoil. Prime Minister Michael Manley was approaching the end of his first term in office, and while his socialist policies were still popular with the Jamaican masses and the Jamaican currency was still strong—hard to believe, but it took about US$1.20 to buy a single JA dollar in those days—the country's economy was fragile. It didn't help that the leader of the Jamaica Labour Party, Edward Seaga, was engaging in firebrand rhetoric, and a meeting of the International Monetary Fund in Kingston early in 1976 had sparked ugly riots in the city's ghetto areas. Manley reacted by bringing in a 7 p.m. curfew in the capital, and the tension was palpable. It was a volatile situation, and it cost many people their lives. Guns were virtually everywhere, and later that year the man who was by now the world's most idolized pop musician was to come close to joining Jamaica's all-too-rapidly growing list of murder victims.

Before that drama would unfold, though, Bob had some touring to take care of.

The Wailers' line-up that flew out of Jamaica in April 1976, headed for the United States, Canada, and Europe, was the most powerful yet. The core members were Bob, Family Man, Carly, Rita, Marcia, and Judy. With them were "Chinna" Smith on rhythm guitar, Donald Kinsey on lead guitar, and "Wya" Lindo and Tyrone Downie, both back in the Wailers' fold after brief absences, on keyboards. This time around, the musicians had even more support: Bob Marley was the hottest commodity in the world of pop music, he could afford to tour in comfort, and the party that left Jamaica included manager Don Taylor, Skill Cole, working in tandem with Taylor as road manager, Antonio "Gilly" Gilbert taking over from Mikey Dan the all-important kitchen duties, sound man Dennis Thompson, artist Neville Garrick, and a backup road manager, Tony "Tony G" Garnett, whose duties included introducing the band on stage. The media blitz that had resulted from the countless interviews Bob sat through at 56 Hope Road paid off handsomely, and the North American leg of the tour was a triumph. The Wailers criss-crossed the United States and Canada, playing to sold-out venues and, as always, ecstatic reviews.

In Los Angeles, where the band had been broke and disheartened just a few years earlier, the Wailers put on the most outstanding show of the tour and one of the greatest of Bob Marley's career. With George Harrison and Ringo Starr among the big names in the audience, the Wailers started the 26 May show at the Roxy with "Trench Town Rock" and continued with fan favorites from *Burnin'* and *Natty Dread* before hitting the audience with "Roots Rock Reggae," "Rat Race," and "Positive Vibration" from the new *Rastaman Vibration* album and finishing with an encore medley of "Get Up Stand Up," "No More Trouble," and "War." The show proved, if any further proof were needed, that Bob Marley was the most compelling, charismatic stage performer in the world.

In June, following the North American leg of the tour, the Wailers headed for Europe—and still more triumphant appearances. After the heady years of the sixties, when groups like the Beatles, the Stones, and the Animals had been making music that mattered, the youth of Europe had become disillusioned with the increasingly glittery and shallow pop scene, and had embraced reggae, with its rebellious and socially conscious message and lively-up-yourself rhythms, wholeheartedly—a love affair that has continued to this day. Bob Marley was their new hero, and he was greeted by adoring crowds in Germany, France, Holland, Wales, and England.

Finally, on record and on tour, Bob Marley, the reggae messenger, had a mass audience hanging on to and singing along with his every word. He was more than just a musician, more than a mere superstar, more, even, than what he aspired to be, an ambassador for Rastafari. People around the world, of all races and all beliefs, were starting to realize that a very special man had appeared in their lifetime.

They had no way of knowing he would almost be snatched away from them before the year was out. And that a seemingly innocuous injury to the big toe on his right foot, sustained that same year while playing soccer at home in Jamaica, would eventually result in the discovery of the deadly cancer that was to cut short his career and his life.

Bob flew back to Jamaica in the early autumn of 1976. It wasn't the sort of homecoming he would have wished for. Jamaica, even by its own volatile standards, was in a situation bordering on anarchy when Bob arrived. The politically motivated violence had escalated to the point where Michael Manley had declared a state of emergency in June, with about five hundred people, many of them prominent supporters of the JLP, arrested and imprisoned —without ever being charged—in the notorious "Gun Court" at the Up-Park Camp military headquarters in Kingston. Many of those who had found themselves behind bars, including Edward Seaga's most trusted aide, Olivia "Babsy" Grange-Walker, felt that they were in so much danger they left the island. She emigrated to Canada, where she managed the careers of prominent reggae artists like Leroy Sibbles, the legendary lead singer of the Heptones, Ernie Smith, and Carlene Davis, and didn't return until Manley was voted out of power in 1980.

Bob Marley, too, wanted to join the fight for Jamaica—with peace his objective and music his weapon of choice.

In October he took the nucleus of the Wailers—minus Donald Kinsey, Chinna, and Wya, and with Family Man adding rhythm guitar and organ to his regular bass guitar duties—into Lee Perry's Black Ark studios to record a hypnotic, almost jazzy, ode to the land of his birth. It was called "Smile Jamaica," and the words— "Smile, you're in Jamaica"— belied the dreadful state the country was in. The same month, he recorded the same song at Harry J's, this time with a horn section and with Neville Garrick and Gilly Gilbert complementing the I-Three on harmony vocals.

Bob, who had been impressed by the success of the charity concert he'd performed with Stevie Wonder a year previously, was keen to do a benefit show himself, partly to say thank you to the people of Jamaica for recognizing, embracing, and supporting him long before he'd become an artist of international stature, partly as a gesture of unity. He wanted to help, in some way, to stop the fighting that was tearing his country apart.

The location was to be National Heroes Park, in the heart of Kingston, but before a concert of that magnitude could take place in a public venue, Bob had to get permission from the government. It was a situation he didn't feel particularly comfortable with— he'd made his suspicion of politicians abundantly clear in the past, both in his lyrics and in interviews—but he had no choice. He was duly given the go-ahead for the Smile Jamaica concert, and the date—5 December—was announced. Almost immediately, Michael Manley called an election for 20 December, a move that inevitably gave the impression that Bob Marley, who had performed on Manley's 1972 campaign bandwagon, was supporting the PNP. And it didn't help when the government announced that the concert was being co-sponsored by the Ministry of Culture.

Almost immediately, people answering the phone at 56 Hope Road started getting threatening messages—and the assumption, naturally enough in the supercharged political climate at the time, was that they were coming from supporters of Edward Seaga's JLP. The fact that political intimidators somehow seemed to be able to get their hands on large numbers of firearms did nothing to calm people's nerves.

Things became so tense that Marcia Griffiths announced unequivocally that she wasn't going to be part of the Smile Jamaica event. Judy Mowatt, too, made her misgivings clear. Bob found himself boxed into an unenviable corner. In good faith, he'd promised the people of Jamaica—his people—that he'd be headlining a free concert in the cause of national unity. There was no way he could let them down, despite his annoyance with the Manley government for making political mileage out of his well-meaning gesture.

Plans for the concert went ahead, and Bob, always the perfectionist, had the Wailers rehearsing constantly at 56 Hope Road in the days leading up to 5 December. On the evening of 3 December, just over forty-eight hours before he was due to make what was sure to be a triumphant appearance before tens of thousands at National Heroes Park, the Wailers were taking a quick break from their unending quest for perfection. Bob was peeling a grapefruit absentmindedly in a room near the front of the sprawling wooden mansion, its door providing open access to the impressive courtyard—the scene of countless impromptu soccer games—that separated the house from Hope Road itself. With him in the room was Wailers guitarist Donald Kinsey.

Suddenly, the tropical night air was shattered by what sounded like firecrackers. It immediately dawned on Bob—a Trench Town survivor—that what he was hearing was gunfire. And, almost before he knew it, this was confirmed as a bullet tore into his left arm, just above the elbow. 56 Hope Road was under attack—a routine evening of rehearsals had turned in a fraction of a second into a nightmare. Bob, almost instinctively, turned sideways, to present as small a target as possible to whoever was firing. Don Taylor, meanwhile, was walking into the same room where Bob had been peeling his grapefruit, wondering what was going on. He quickly found out. His route took him directly across the door from where the shots were coming, and five bullets struck him in the side, the upper leg and around the groin area. Taylor collapsed, bleeding, while Marley and Kinsey tried to keep themselves out of the line of fire.

In the room next door, the scene was equally chaotic. There was more than one gunman, the shooting was intense, and Family Man and the rest of the band, trying frantically to avoid the bullets, were crowding as best they could into an adjoining bathroom. One of the shots grazed Rita Marley's head. Still more severely wounded was Louis Simpson, a friend of the Wailers who had the misfortune of hanging out at 56 Hope Road that fateful evening. For a few seconds it seemed that a massacre was inevitable. Bullets flew everywhere—in the kitchen, the bathroom, the living room.

Then, almost as suddenly as it started, the firing stopped. The gunmen—some eyewitnesses said there were as many as seven of them, all teenagers—piled into the cars that they'd driven, unchecked, into 56 Hope Road a few minutes earlier, and roared through the gates. For minutes, everyone in the house remained stunned, not sure who was alive, who was wounded, uncertain what to do, wondering if the ambush in the night was really over or if some of the gunmen had remained to finish what they'd started. Finally, the wounded—Don Taylor, Bob, Rita and Louis Simpson—were rushed to the hospital.

Most of the unscathed members of the band, badly shaken and frightened for their lives, went their separate ways, leaving Family Man and Tyrone Downie to deal with the police.

Chris Blackwell and Jeff Walker, the publicity director for Island Records, were on the scene soon after the drama, along with long-time Wailers friend Dickie Jobson. The three had been at the Sheraton hotel when they heard of the shooting, and while they were driving at top speed to 56 Hope Road the news was confirmed on the car radio. After a quick survey of the damage at Hope Road, they rushed to the hospital, where they discovered that Prime Minister Michael Manley was already there, along with various Jamaican VIPs. Sitting in the corner, with his left arm bandaged and still wearing a blood-covered shirt, was Bob Marley. Doctors had decided it would be too dangerous to remove the bullet that had lodged in his arm, and it was to remain there for the rest of his life. Don Taylor, who had been declared in critical condition, was operated on almost immediately, and later flown to Miami for further surgery. The anxious gathering was still awaiting word on Rita. It turned out that she was in no danger from the graze to her head, but the hospital decided she should stay overnight for observation.

The motivation for the shooting and the identities of the gunmen remain a mystery to this day. There have been almost as many theories as there were bullets fired on that fateful night, but Neville Garrick, who had left 56 Hope Road not long before the onslaught began, to drive Judy Mowatt home to Bull Bay, describes it as "one of the great unsolved crimes in history."

The immediate suspicion was that it might be a politically motivated assassination attempt by supporters of the Jamaica Labour Party, angered by the upcoming Smile Jamaica concert and what they perceived to be Bob's support for Michael Manley. But why, people wondered, would the thugs allied to the JLP risk the political backlash that would be the inevitable result if they'd succeeded in killing Bob Marley, who was far and away the best-loved man in Jamaica?

Another theory was that Bob's closest friend, Skill Cole, had crossed members of the Jamaican equivalent of the Mob in a race-course scam, and that the shooting had been their way of sending a message to whoever was at 56 Hope Road that they weren't people to be messed with.

In New York, meanwhile, the extraordinary PR man Charles Comer had decided instantly that whatever the truth of the matter might be, the story Marley fans around the world would read and hear was that Jamaica's turbulent politics were behind the nightmare at 56 Hope Road. Comer spent most of the next two days phoning newspapers and TV and radio stations around the world with this version of the story—and for many years a failed assassination attempt by unknown gunmen was the commonly accepted account of what had taken place.

Decades later, the indefatigable Comer was to confess to close friends that it was the only time in his long career that he deliberately lied to the press about an artist he was working for. "I couldn't have people around the world thinking the great Bob Marley, their idol, might be involved in some way with something as tacky as a racecourse scam," said Comer. "It would have ruined Bob's reputation. To me, the assassination theory was the only story we could possibly have people believe. I didn't give a fuck. I wasn't going to have Bob Marley's name associated in any way with something that wasn't honest."

Even while they breathed a collective sigh of relief that Bob had survived an assassination attempt, fans around the world were stunned by his brush with death. So was Bob himself. Why, he wondered, would someone want to shoot him? Who were they? Would they try again? Was he still in danger? Should he risk his life by performing at National Heroes Park on 5 December, less than two days away?

It was obvious that Bob had to go into hiding as soon as possible. But where? His face was the best-known in Jamaica, and it would have been pointless, and perhaps highly dangerous, for him to stay anywhere in or around Kingston. It was quickly decided that the safest place would be a remote Great House high in the mountains overlooking Kingston, owned by Chris Blackwell, and Bob was immediately driven up the tortuous, winding road to Blackwell's hideaway. It's called Strawberry Hill, and the original house, which was destroyed by Hurricane Gilbert in 1988, has been replaced by a cluster of ultra-chic, pastel-hued cottages catering to well-heeled travelers looking for a Jamaican experience that's vastly different from the tourist areas of the island's North Coast.

For a couple of days between 3 and 5 December in 1976, Strawberry Hill became virtually an armed camp, with gun-toting police patrolling its perimeters and Bob's Rasta bredren lurking in the dense forests and bush on both sides of the road that is the only access to the estate, their razor-edged machetes at the ready if any gunmen were foolish enough to try to finish what they'd started.

He had survived the shooting, but Bob was left to face an agonizing decision: should he go ahead with the Smile Jamaica concert? Island Records' Jeff Walker drove up to Strawberry Hill the afternoon after the shooting. He says there seemed to be no way that the show would go on. Bob was wounded, Don Taylor was still in a critical condition, Rita was in the hospital, and the Wailers had scattered to various points in and around Kingston. Strawberry Hill wasn't a happy place, and Bob Marley wasn't a happy man.

As the afternoon turned to night, various Rasta elders showed up at Strawberry Hill, along with Bob's friend Cat Coore, the lead guitarist of Third World. Then the news reached Strawberry Hill that Don Taylor had been airlifted to Miami for further surgery, and that Rita was doing well. Spliffs were lit, and the small gathering got down to serious reasoning.

Says Jeff Walker: "The overwhelming sentiment at that time was that Bob would be crazy to go down."

But Walker felt differently. He was more than a little intimidated by the heavyweight gathering of some of Jamaica's most prominent Rasta elders, but decided he would have his say anyway, and told Bob that if he decided not to perform, the gunmen would have achieved at least one of their objectives—to stop the music. Walker recalls that Bob replied, "There's no way I'm going on stage without a machine gun."

Walker's response was, by his own admission, corny: "Your guitar's your machine gun, Bob." It drew some laughter from the gathering, but they also seemed to accept that Walker had made some valid points, and by the time everyone had retired for the night, with the concert less than twenty-four hours away, no firm decision had been made. The concert wasn't on . . . but at least it wasn't off.

The following morning, the general feeling was that Bob would perform. This sentiment was reinforced that afternoon by reports from National Heroes Park that thousands of people were turning up, and that the vibes were positive. By six o'clock, the crowd had reached an estimated fifty thousand—but Bob still hadn't finally made his mind up.

Before long, Third World were on stage and playing, as much to test the mood as keep the crowd entertained, and Bob seemed to be more and more leaning toward playing. Then a trusted Manley associate, Housing Minister Tony Spaulding, turned up with a group that included the Commissioner of Police. They were in three cars and had been sent to escort Bob to the event. By now, it looked almost certain that the concert would take place —and then Rita appeared, her head bandaged and still wearing her hospital robe. She vehemently disagreed with Bob risking his life by playing, and quickly made her feelings known. Once again the Smile Jamaica concert was in the balance. Suddenly, Bob made up his mind. He would perform. He and Rita—still in the hospital gown—jumped in a car with Tony Spaulding and sped off down the hair-raising mountainside road to Kingston, a car full of armed policemen leading the convoy, Bob's group in the center, and Jeff Walker and the Commissioner of Police, who was busily assembling a small machine gun, bringing up the rear.

By the time they reached National Heroes Park the crowd had swollen to an estimated eighty thousand, one of the biggest single gatherings of people ever in Jamaica. When Bob finally reached the stage he looked out at the sea of faces. One of the first things he saw, about ten yards away, was Michael Manley sitting on top of a van, making himself, quite deliberately, a highly visible target for any gunmen who might be in the midst of the massive crowd. Manley's message was clear: if Bob Marley was willing to risk his life for the people of Jamaica, so was their Prime Minister.

Bob had planned to do only a couple of numbers—which, in the circumstances, no one could have complained about. His first song was an inspired choice—"War." Another inspired choice followed—"No More Trouble." The couple of songs soon became three, then four, then, with the first live performance of "Smile Jamaica," five. Bob eventually played for an hour and a half before winding up with "So Jah Seh," showing his wounds pointedly to the crowd, and dashing off stage. It was one of the greatest performances of his career—and one of the last live appearances he would make in Jamaica.

Bob was quickly spirited back up to Strawberry Hill, but by now he'd decided he didn't want to risk staying any longer than he had to on his violence-plagued island, and a charter jet was arranged to fly him to the Bahamas.

Around 6:30 a.m. on 7 December, Bob Marley, accompanied by Neville Garrick, was driven from Strawberry Hill to Norman Manley Airport, where a private jet awaited them. A few minutes later it took off . . . carrying Bob to Nassau and fourteen months of self-imposed exile from the land of his birth.

During that period he would tour extensively, write some of his most brilliant songs and record the album *Time* magazine was to acclaim as the greatest of the twentieth century. He'd also spend more and more time with Cindy Breakspeare, who by now had been crowned Miss World.

It was to be a busy exile.

Is This Love...Bob with Cindy Breakspeare at 56 Hope Road

13.

Movement of Jah People

When Bob Marley and Neville Garrick landed in the Bahamas their welcome was less than warm. At the best of times, the staid and conservative Bahamas wasn't the most welcoming of places for a couple of dreadlocked Rastas—even if they were on a fancy chartered jet, and even if one of them was the most exalted figure in all of popular music and the other was a superbly talented artist with a degree from one of America's most prestigious universities. It didn't help that the Bahamian authorities knew who Bob Marley was and had heard all about the bloodshed at 56 Hope Road only a few days earlier. First they asked him sternly if he and his companion were seeking political asylum. It was an obvious ploy to have him say yes and then send the two of them packing. It didn't dawn on the officials—it seldom did in those days when overly zealous bureaucrats were dealing with Rastas—that they were trying to outfox one of the smartest human beings on the planet, a man who'd survived living rough in Trench Town, who'd negotiated the treacherous world of the Jamaican music business and made it to the cover of the *Rolling Stone*, who'd outwitted scores of intrusive journalists hell bent on making him say something they could sensationalize and that he'd later regret.

"No, me is a tourist," replied Bob.

Catering to well-heeled tourists is the Bahamas' main business, and the two dreads had just landed in a private jet, so the Bahamian authorities had little choice but, somewhat reluctantly, to let Bob and Neville into the country. Fortunately, the two were also able to tell the authorities that they had somewhere to stay— once again, Chris Blackwell was to provide the accommodation. Bob and Neville headed for his Bahamas cottage home, Sea Pussy.

After the drama the weary pair had just been through in Kingston, the laid-back Bahamas suited them just fine, and around mid-morning they finally managed to catch a little sleep. And a little sleep it was. After two or three hours they were awakened by Bahamian immigration authorities and taken back to the airport, where they were grilled about the shooting at 56 Hope Road. Eventually they were given a visa, but it was only for a week. Then they had to get it renewed, but only for another week. The following week it was the same routine. As Neville Garrick was to recall, they stayed in the Bahamas for three weeks and had to get three separate visas. After a few days Bob and Neville were joined by Rita, three of her and Bob's kids, and most of the rest of the Wailers, who had been only too eager to get out of Jamaica, where they believed, not unreasonably, that their lives were still in danger.

Bob Marley spent his time in the Bahamas reflecting on the horrific events in Jamaica, chilling by the pool—and writing new songs. It was the start of what was perhaps the most creative period of his life. It was in the Bahamas that he started work on a song that would be one of many outstanding numbers on *Survival*, an album that was released more than two years later and which many Wailers fans still insist was Bob's finest, despite *Time* magazine's choice of *Exodus* as the best album of the twentieth century. The song, inspired by the horrific events at 56 Hope Road, was to be called "Ambush in the Night."

After three weeks, though, it was time for Bob and the Wailers to move on—and it had been decided the best place for them to move on to would be London. Their earliest experiences in the crowded and damp English capital hadn't been particularly pleasant, but since then the Wailers had come to enjoy the city. It didn't hurt that they were now in a position to live in comfort. The availability of excellent recording facilities, courtesy of Island Records, was another significant plus, as was the UK music scene, which hadn't been as vibrant since the early days of the Beatles and the Stones. Up-and-coming young British reggae bands like Aswad, Black Slate, and Steel Pulse were starting to make a name for themselves, following hard on the heels of the trail-blazing Matumbi and Cimarons, while white Britain was being shaken to its staid roots by a phenomenon called punk, spearheaded by the anarchic Sex Pistols and a hugely talented band called the Clash—the latter capable of playing some downright wicked dub.

If all of that wasn't enough, London had a couple of other things going for it. England was much, much safer than Jamaica —the cops didn't even carry guns. For another thing, Cindy Breakspeare, Bob's main—but by no means only—love interest at the time would be living there, carrying out her obligations as the reigning Miss World.

Already well known in Jamaica as one of the island's most beautiful women, the Canadian-born Breakspeare—her mother is Canadian, her father Jamaican—had taken part in the Miss World contest in England the previous month, and had won the crown (the show was compered by another famous Bob—this one with the surname Hope). Cindy had met Bob Marley early in 1975, when he and his Rasta posse had more or less taken over 56 Hope Road, where she was sharing a downstairs apartment with her brother, Reds. Their initial acquaintance had blossomed into a torrid affair—a development that had scandalized Jamaica's elitist and largely racist uptown society. Bob Marley, who had been spurned by the black relatives of a girl he'd fallen in love with in Trench Town more than a decade earlier because his skin was too fair, wouldn't have missed the irony of being just as emphatically rejected by the fair-skinned Jamaicans who populated the world in which Cindy Breakspeare lived. Years later, in an interview with Roger Steffens, Cindy spoke of the uproar their relationship had sparked in her upper-crusty circle: "When I got involved with Bob the uptown folks were outraged. They were outraged! I mean, they've come to accept him today as a man who has attained the Order of Merit in Jamaica, and so there's a level of respect there for his creativity and the mark that he made on the world. But back in those days people thought I was absolutely crazy. Absolutely crazy! Is he clean? Is his hair clean? Does he smell? And those were just some of the petty things they could find to focus on. So it was really quite outrageous. Uptown girls were not going out with

Rastafarians, and they certainly were not having babies for them. I mean, that was a whole social revolution in Jamaica. I have girlfriends who tell me today that their parents sat them down on the couch in the living room and said, 'Now listen, you see what Cindy has done? Don't even think about it!'"

She also spoke of Bob's somewhat unorthodox—though clearly effective—courting technique in those early days at 56 Hope Road. "He would go by the door and kind of glance sideways to see if anybody was around, and attempt to engage me in conversation, and of course it would always be philosophy and talking about how you see yourself, how you present yourself as a woman and all the things you should and shouldn't do, because of course doctrine was everything then. And he would sit on the steps out the back of my apartment there with a guitar and sing. I remember hearing 'Turn Your Lights Down Low' just like that. And he wasn't a man of words on a one-to-one basis, you know, not a lot. And certainly not when he was just getting to know somebody, he was very shy that way. And his gestures were very innocent and very boyish. He would offer a mango as a gift, or simple little things like that, which I thought were very charming, especially since I had been involved with people whose style was quite different. I found it very disarming."

The Wailers were in a much more optimistic frame of mind by the time their Heathrow-bound British Airways jet left Nassau in early January 1977. The first item on the agenda was to find somewhere to live—and this time it wouldn't be a tacky, rundown hotel in a dodgy area, or a nondescript house in the far-flung suburbs. They found it quickly, on Oakley Street in London's trendy and expensive Chelsea district, just around the corner from the ultra-chic King's Road. Dating back to the 1850s, Oakley Street is lined with elegant Victorian houses, and the Wailers quickly rented Number 42, a spacious four-story terraced house with ample room for all of them.

Their presence in London was still a closely guarded secret—to all intents and purposes, one of the planet's most famous musicians and his band had dropped off the face of the earth. After the trauma they'd lived through in Kingston, all Bob Marley and the Wailers wanted to do was keep the lowest of profiles and make music.

For two months that's exactly what they did. It was only when a British journalist who specialized in writing about reggae bumped into Bob and Neville in Chelsea that the band's presence in London became public knowledge, and by then the recording of the album that was to be called *Exodus*, and which would catapult Bob to the next level of global fame and adulation, was well under way.

The only thing missing when the Wailers set up camp in London was a lead guitarist. Al Anderson was playing and recording with Peter Tosh. Dodging bullets at 56 Hope Road had been more than enough JA-style drama for Donald Kinsey, and he had returned to the States (he too would soon join Peter's crack Word, Sound and Power band). And, although it offended some reggae "purists," who thought rock or blues-style guitar solos had no place in reggae, Bob Marley was convinced—as he had been since Wayne Perkins's memorable overdubs on "Concrete Jungle" five years earlier—that the purists were wrong. Not that he cared, one way or another. Bob always maintained that music was free, and that as a musician he was free to do what he wanted, when he wanted and with whom he wanted. And what he wanted in early 1977 was a guitarist to fill the void left by the back-to-back departures of Anderson and Kinsey.

Once again, it was Chris Blackwell who stepped up to the plate and hit a home run. And once again, the Wailers would have a lead guitarist whose musical roots weren't Jamaican. Julian "Junior" Marvin had been born in Jamaica, mind you, but had been sent to live in England when he was nine. By the time he was introduced to Bob Marley his reputation was as a brilliant guitarist on two fronts: the American R 'n' B and the London rock scenes. Equally important, being Jamaican by birth, he came with a deep-rooted, second-nature feel for reggae, even if he'd rarely played it.

Marvin's professional music career had started as a keyboardist —a role he'd filled with a band called the Nighttimers, whose leader was the brilliant guitarist John McLaughlin. The multi-talented Marvin soon switched to the guitar after hearing people like McLaughlin, Jimi Hendrix, and Eric Clapton, and it was as a guitarist that he acquired his heaviest credentials, moving to the States for a while and playing with T-Bone Walker, Ike and Tina Turner, and Billy Preston. Then he returned to England, where he soon met Chris Wood from the hugely successful English rock band Traffic—fronted by a now grown-up Stevie Winwood and part of Chris Blackwell's Island stable. Marvin was recruited to play on Winwood's massive *Arc of a Diver* album, which brought him, in turn, to the attention of Blackwell, who soon had him in the studio doing session work with the legendary Toots and the Maytals, another Island act at the time, whose brand of reggae had a funky, bluesy feel ideally suited to Junior's style of playing.

When Blackwell introduced him to Bob Marley as a potential replacement for Al Anderson and Donald Kinsey, Marvin was already a Marley fan—albeit a closet one. Years later, he was to recall his first close encounter with the Wailers: "I'd heard 'Concrete Jungle' and I liked the guitar solo on there. I kind of wished I was playing with a band like that, so I was definitely a fan. In fact, I saw them in the studio, Island Studio on Basing Street. I'm not sure if they were doing *Natty Dread* or *Burnin'* or *Catch a Fire* but they were there and they were talking about what instrumentation to put on a certain track. And I watched them from outside the door but I never went in. I didn't really have the nerve to go in and introduce myself. Then I saw them perform at a club called the Speakeasy and they were phenomenal."

When Blackwell arranged a meeting between Junior and Bob early in 1977, there was an instant rapport. Almost before he knew it, Junior Marvin's most cherished musical ambition had become a reality: he was a Wailer. And he would remain one well into the twenty-first century, decades after Bob's passing.

The Wailers welcomed the new guitarist, without hesitation and without reservation, into their tightly knit family. Brilliant musicians themselves, they knew, almost instinctively, that Junior Marvin was right for their sound. And while he didn't talk like a Jamaican, it didn't hurt that Jamaica was where he'd been born and where his roots were. Almost before he knew what was happening,

Marvin found himself in Island Records' London studios, recording a track that was soon to become an international anthem. The song was called "Exodus," and it would be the title track of Bob Marley's upcoming album. A somewhat radical departure from conventional reggae, "Exodus" was more strident, more rocky, more in the intense groove of "War" from *Rastaman Vibration.* And Junior Marvin's lead guitar fitted right into that groove. He played on that epic track with commendable economy—there'd be plenty of time for extravagant solos during live performances of "Exodus" in the months and years ahead—his almost percussive guitar complementing the militant riddim laid down by Family Man and Carly, and towards the end of the song his guitar took on an almost vocal quality, virtually echoing, instrumentally, Bob's repeated refrain: "Movement of Jah people."

As a bonus, Junior Marvin brought his friend Roger Mayer, the world's foremost guitar guru, into the Wailers' camp. Mayer, who had been the guitar-tuning genius behind Jimi Hendrix, added a new dimension to the already finely honed Wailers sound. Recalls Junior: "Roger showed us how to keep the guitars in tune and how to adjust them and set the harmonics—and the tone of the guitar and the bass, how important it was. He worked on Bob's guitar. He worked on my guitar. And having worked with Jimi Hendrix, he pretty much was the guitar man. Everybody wanted him. I was so lucky that he even cared to want to organize my guitar for me. And I told Bob about him and Bob said, 'Yeah, we gotta get him!' He came and helped pick out some of the actual tones for some of the songs and helped me set up the pedals and everything. It made a difference because he was so way ahead of everybody where that was concerned. All the guitars sound right. They were perfectly in tune and everything. Notes are just coming out very harmonious. And I think that made a big difference, due to the fact that reggae actually became more in harmony. The melodies became stronger because everything was so perfectly in tune. Back then, people weren't aware of guitar tuners and stuff like that. A lot of people tuned by ear and sometimes it could be a little bit off. Especially in Jamaica, where they were a bit behind in instrumentation and new technology. Therefore, a lot of the reggae records before that were slightly out of tune but it still sounded good. 'Exodus' was just perfect."

The rest of the tracks on the *Exodus* album were well nigh perfect too.

The first side of the epic album (this was in the long-ago days, before CDs, when albums had two sides) consisted of songs with a powerful message. Side Two was lighter, an infectious mix of uptempo, uplifting tunes and a couple of gorgeous love songs.

The opening notes of the first track on *Exodus*, "Natural Mystic," were particularly memorable—because they could barely be heard. For a few seconds after lowering the needle into the lead-in grooves (that's what you did in the days of vinyl), there was nothing. Then, almost imperceptibly, Tyrone Downie's organ, playing a single, simple chord, insinuated itself into your consciousness. A couple of seconds later, Family Man's bass and Carly's delicate high-hat joined in, but they too were barely audible. The bass line was intriguing, insistent . . . but could Fams possibly be playing so quietly? What was going on here? There was only one thing to do: crank up the volume. Ah, that's better. Wait a minute, though, it's getting louder . . . and louder . . . and louder. After about twenty-five seconds, it was full watts tonight, and your neighbors were being well and truly disturbed. Then a whiplash drum roll from Carly, and, finally, that voice. "There's a natural mystic, blowing through the air, if you listen carefully now you will hear . . ."

The three tracks that followed "Natural Mystic"— "So Much Things To Say," "Guiltiness," "The Heathen"— were Bob Marley at his most righteous, an exhortation to beware of the evils of mankind. He sang of spiritual wickedness in high and low places, of guiltiness resting 'pon the conscience of evil-doers, of heathens' backs against the wall. Popular music had never sounded like this. It was a thunderous, conscious-raising sermon . . . and you could skank to it.

Then the finale on Side One: "Exodus," the movement of Jah people. You'd been through tribulation, and Bob Marley and the Wailers were going to take you to a better place, to a promised land.

With Side Two, you were there. Now you were "Jamming," like you'd never jammed before. You didn't want to be "Waiting in Vain" for love, and you didn't have to. By the next track, possibly the most beautiful love song ever written, it was time to "Turn Your Lights Down Low," to close your window curtain, to let Jah light shine in. If you weren't feeling pretty good by now, "Three Little Birds" would lift your spirits, just as they'd lifted Bob's when they'd perched on a window ledge at 56 Hope Road. Finally, exultantly, "One Love." Let's get together and feel alright.

Bob Marley was on a creative roll unequalled in the history of popular music. The ten tracks that made up Exodus were chosen from twice that number recorded at the same landmark sessions. The rest, most of them considerably more relaxed and meditative than the *Exodus* tracks, would be saved for Bob's next album, *Kaya*, which wouldn't be released until the following year.

Between rehearsing and recording, Bob was spending most of his time contentedly at 42 Oakley Street, along with his band and bredren from the vibrant London Rasta scene, transforming a trendy London street into a dreadlock camp and raising the eyebrows of his Chelsea neighbors, just as he'd done with the uptown crowd in the vicinity of 56 Hope Road when he'd moved in a couple of years earlier. His almost constant companion was Cindy Breakspeare, but he still found time to play plenty of soccer. With Bob Marley, music came first, but there was always time for soccer, for his Bible, and for love.

There was also of course always time for herb—and it led to one of the most infamous, albeit humorous, incidents during the recording of *Exodus*. It happened one evening when the band was about to leave Island's Basing Street studios. They were being driven home by Neville Garrick, who'd been away for most of the evening. He'd just returned to the studio and was dismayed when he was told there was no herb left—not so much as a tiny joint, much less a Jamaican-style spliff. Outside the studio, the crowd of dreads caught the attention of a passing police car, whose occupants promptly decided—these were the days of Britain's infamous "suss" law—to search the Rastas and their car for marijuana.

Soccer was among Marley's passions. Here he launches a long pass into opposition territory.

To Neville's disgust, they found spliffs tucked away in Fams's socks and Bob's pockets. Not only was he being busted, he was being busted for herb he'd just been solemnly assured didn't exist. The incident ended harmlessly enough, with Bob, who'd told the cops the herb was all his, being fined £30.

With the *Exodus* sessions completed, and that epic album about to be released, it was time once more for touring. Bob and the band hadn't been on the road since mid-1976, and they were keen to showcase their new material live. And the new Wailer, Junior Marvin, having proved himself in the studio, was perhaps the keenest of them all. He wanted to show his new musical comrades what he could do on stage as well. Dates were arranged in France, Holland, Germany, Sweden, and Denmark, a large, comfortable bus was booked, and the Wailers were on the road again.

The first concert was in Paris, in May. As usual, the tour itinerary had to include soccer—these dates were almost as important as the shows themselves. During the obligatory match in Paris, an opposing player, tackling Bob, came down hard with his studs on Bob's right foot. The result was a nasty wound to his big toe—by an ugly coincidence in exactly the same place Bob had suffered an injury in 1976, during a match in Trench Town. That wound had never properly healed, and Bob had never bothered to see a doctor—he'd dealt with it the West Indian way, cleaning it with cotton and dousing it with stinging antiseptic. In Paris, Bob did go to a doctor, who removed the nail of Bob's right big toe and told him to stay off his feet for a while. It was just what he didn't want to hear at the start of a major tour supporting a new album and, predictably, he ignored the doctor's advice. He continued the tour with a bandage on his right foot, and continued to perform magnificently . . . even though he'd sometimes find the wound had bled into his shoe during a performance. Bob Marley may have been the world's biggest star, but he was still at heart a tough youth from Trench Town by way of country. An injury to his big toe wasn't going to stop him doing what he was destined to do. He even continued to play soccer.

In every other way the tour was a triumph. And by the time the Wailers returned to London, for a series of concerts at the venerable Rainbow Theatre in Finsbury Park, *Exodus* was well on its way to becoming the biggest-selling Bob Marley album yet. The Rainbow shows were historic in every way. Almost twenty-five years later, with the twentieth century drawing to a close, a video of one of them was buried in a time capsule in a vault beneath the New York Times Building in Manhattan, not to be opened until the dawn of the year 3000. It was, the august newspaper decided, the finest possible example of twentieth-century culture for generations a thousand years from now to contemplate, enjoy, and appreciate.

Bob's foot, meanwhile, stubbornly refused to heal. And he stubbornly refused to take it easy, to give it time to get better. To stop dancing like a man possessed on stage, to stop playing soccer as though he were in a World Cup final against Brazil.

In late July 1977 another distraction appeared in the midst of the busy London runnings: Lee "Scratch" Perry. Like Bob, Scratch was intrigued by the London punk scene, and the two soon found themselves in Island's studios, recording a number celebrating reggae's affinity with the rebellious punk movement. It was called "Punky Reggae Party," and, with Scratch at the controls, Bob was accompanied by an intriguing assortment of musicians, with not a Wailer among them. They included Third World's Cat Coore and Ibo Cooper, along with Aswad's Angus Gaye. At the same session Bob recorded an updated version of "Keep On Moving" from the Wailers' 1971 Lee Perry era, this time full of messages for his children back in Jamaica. "Tell Auntie I'm fine and to keep Cedella in line," he sang, the auntie in question being Rita's redoubtable Aunt Viola, who had kicked him out of her house all those years ago and who was now looking after his and Rita's kids while their parents were recording in London.

Following Bob's musical reunion with Scratch, the Wailers were due for another major tour, this time in the United States. But Bob's wounded and abused right foot was getting worse, not better, and soon he was barely able to walk. Reluctantly, the doctor-wary Bob finally decided he should see a specialist. He couldn't perform on stage, he could no longer play soccer, something was clearly not right. He arranged to see a foot specialist in London's renowned Harley Street, and the news couldn't have been worse: the doctor had detected cancer cells in his big toe. Worse still, it was melanoma, a potentially deadly form of skin cancer. Bob was told he should have the toe and part of his right foot amputated to prevent the malignant cells from invading the rest of his body. Bob was stunned, and his mother, Cedella, recalls the anguished phone call she received in the States. "Mamma, I never do nobody no evil. I never do nobody no wrong. Why would Jah give me cancer?"

It was a question she couldn't answer.

Bob's Rasta beliefs wouldn't allow amputation. And he didn't want to die—life, he often said, was the most precious gift of all, and he was in the prime of his, an international star of immense stature, a global messenger for Rastafari, a benefactor to thousands of his beloved ghetto people back in Jamaica. He decided to seek a second opinion, and flew to Miami, where Dr. William Bacon advised him that part of his toe would have to be cut away, but not actually amputated, along with some of the flesh higher up the foot. The American tour was promptly cancelled—to the dismay of some in the Wailers camp who put profits ahead of health, a stance that angered Marley immensely. Bob was operated on in Miami's Cedars of Lebanon Hospital. The nail of his right big toe was once again removed, along with some of the adjacent flesh, and skin from his thigh area grafted onto the wounded foot. At first it seemed as though the operation was a success. Sadly, it wasn't; Bob Marley was to die in that same hospital less than four years later.

With *Exodus* selling briskly despite the cancelled tour, Bob flew back to London to recuperate from the operation—and into the waiting and welcoming arms of Cindy Breakspeare. The healing process, both mental and physical, had started. In the weeks and months after the operation, Cindy recalled, Bob had every reason to be optimistic. "It healed really, really beautifully, and he used to take good care of it and everything. It really healed well and he wouldn't allow it to get injured in any way. The skin over it of course was very tender, having been taken from the leg, the upper thigh area. So it wasn't quite like the skin that would be on the toe. It was softer, so one needed to be careful, what shoes you wore and everything, so nothing irritated it and rubbed on it too much, but it healed beautifully."

With his toe apparently on the mend, Bob Marley got on with his busy life, writing music, hanging with his bredren, and returning, once again, to Miami, where he'd just bought a spacious new home for his mother. Cedella's beloved Mr. Booker had died, and Bob had decided it was time for her to escape the cold of Delaware. He spent several weeks there, and during that time returned to Cedars of Lebanon for a check-up on his foot. The news was good: he was assured the operation had successfully removed the cancerous cells. "The news left us giddy with joy," says his mother.

It was during this period that he first learned of a concert that was being planned for the following year in Jamaica, a concert that was being organized by some of his long-time bredren from the ghetto areas of Kingston.

It was to be a concert in the cause of peace. And there was only one man who could headline it.

14.
The Peace Concert

Bob Marley headlined many historic concerts during his all too brief career: at the Lyceum in London, where the classic live version of "No Woman No Cry" was recorded; at the Rainbow in London, the show immortalized in the time capsule buried beneath the New York Times Building in Manhattan; at the Roxy in L.A.; at Zimbabwe's independence celebrations in 1980; at the legendary Amandla event in Boston that same year; at the Carib Theatre in Kingston, where Bob, Peter, and Bunny blew away soul great Marvin Gaye and his thirty-piece orchestra; at the San Siro soccer stadium in Milan, where Bob and his conquering Rasta lions played before more than 100,000 ecstatic fans, outdrawing the Pope and setting an attendance record that still stands in Italy; at the Speakeasy, in London, in the days when the Wailers were just starting to go "outernational"; at the Apollo, the hallowed shrine of black culture in the heart of Harlem.

But the most historic—the concert that would forever define Bob Marley's stature as a symbol of peace and universal brotherhood, and confirm, beyond any reasonable doubt, his status as one of the greatest figures ever to emerge from the melting pot of humanity we call the Caribbean—was the Peace Concert in Jamaica's National Stadium in April 1978.

The concert was conceived in the most unlikely of places and by the most unlikely of people: in a prison cell, by two notorious ghetto warlords. Sharing the cell were two senior members of opposing Jamaican political gangs, Claudius "Claudie" Massop and Bucky Marshall. They were among scores of known gunmen being rounded up on sight by the army, which had been called in by Prime Minister Michael Manley to patrol the streets of Kingston to combat an unprecedented wave of murders, rapes, and looting. The pair were ghetto "dons," Massop aligned with the JLP and Marshall with the PNP. Massop was decidedly the heavier of these two rankin' street warlords, and, given the volatile situation in Jamaica at the time, the potential for unpleasantness when they found themselves sharing the same few square feet was considerable. Instead, they started to "reason"—and soon concluded that the wholesale slaughter in which they were heavily involved was pointless. They and their ghetto bredren were putting their lives on the line daily, and for what? So one politician could cling to power? So another politician could seize power? They were all pawns in a brutal political game, and as the slaughter escalated in Kingston's ghettos it was clear that their lives counted for little or nothing so far as their political masters were concerned. But what could they do to try to stop the violence? It would have to be something symbolic, a grand gesture that would unite Jamaicans of all political stripes. They agreed that a huge concert dedicated to the cause of national peace and unity might have a chance of succeeding. It had been tried before, they knew, but the Smile Jamaica concert had been virtually hijacked and turned into a political gambit by Michael Manley's PNP, and the memory of Bob Marley's brush with death was still fresh in the minds of every Jamaican.

This time, they decided, they'd distance the event from the tribal wars. It would be a concert for the people, by the people. And there was only one man who could headline it and make it work: Bob Marley. But Bob was still in exile—he hadn't set foot in Jamaica since flying out of the island four days after the infamous shooting at 56 Hope Road in December 1976, and he was now living mainly in London. Massop, though, was an old spar of Marley's, a friendship that went back to their days as teenagers in Trench Town. He knew Bob would listen to what he had to say. In February 1978, after being released from prison, Massop flew to London along with fellow ghetto warlords and long-time Marley bredren, Tony Welsh and Earl "Tek Life" Wadley. They quickly arranged a meeting with Bob and made their pitch. Appropriately enough, this took place during the shooting of the wonderful *Is This Love* video, which was being filmed in north London at the Keskidee Centre, a former church transformed into a black cultural center that occupied a revered place in the heart and soul of Britain's black community. In the video, Bob, looking almost radiantly happy, assumes the role of a musical Pied Piper, singing and dancing amid a horde of excited and exuberant children (among them two bright young girls who would find their own fame and fortune in the world of fashion many years later: the model Naomi Campbell and the designer Stella McCartney, the latter the daughter of another rather well-known musician, Sir Paul McCartney).

The ghetto dons made Bob Marley an offer he couldn't refuse: the opportunity to help bring peace to the streets of Jamaica. Bob, always decisive, wasted little time in making up his mind: if the concert they were pitching to him could help save lives, maybe even bring a lasting peace to his country, he had to be part of it. He said he'd return to Jamaica to headline the event. The video he was shooting at the time and the title of one of the most popular tracks from the album *Exodus*, by now bubbling on the charts on both sides of the Atlantic, jointly helped give birth to the formal title of the momentous occasion: it would be called the One Love Concert for Peace. The date was quickly confirmed: 22 April 1978, to coincide with the twelfth anniversary of the visit to Jamaica of His Imperial Majesty Haile Selassie I of Ethiopia, King of Kings, Lord of Lords, Conquering Lion of the Tribe of Judah. Bob hadn't been in Jamaica for that moment in history, but he would be there to mark its anniversary. It was to be a special happening.

Soon the official announcement of the historic concert was made—and wire services jumped on the story. But the version they were carrying wasn't entirely accurate. The concert, it was announced, would be a reunion of the original Wailers: Bob Marley, Peter Tosh, and Bunny Wailer were to play together again at Kingston's National Stadium in the cause of peace. Within days, scores of Wailers fans around the world were making plans to be in Kingston. It might be dangerous, but they weren't about to miss the chance to be part of history in the making.

As it turned out, the Wailers' reunion didn't take place—and it never would. But what did happen was every bit as momentous, every bit as historic, as eager fans of the Wailers could have hoped for.

Bob Marley flew back to Jamaica on 26 February 1978. It was almost fourteen months since he'd left his island, and the country he returned to was not a happy place. Kingston, and particularly its ghetto areas, was under the gun. People were being shot and killed on an almost daily basis—many of them innocent bystanders who found themselves in the wrong place at the wrong time as warring gangs opened fire on each other. Bob's return couldn't have been more timely: if ever a Caribbean island needed a peacemaker, it was Jamaica in early 1978. Bob quickly settled back into his usual Jamaican routine. There were joyous and bois-terous reunions with Rasta bredren, much slapping of hands and burning of spliffs. Soccer and endless intense rehearsals were once again the main items on the agenda at 56 Hope Road. Natty Dread was home.

As plans for the Peace Concert were being finalized, it quickly became apparent that the anticipated reunion of the Wailers wasn't going to happen. Peter Tosh agreed to perform, but as a solo act. Bunny Wailer, cynical of the fledgling Peace Movement's chances of success, wanted no part of it. But, as compensation, many other outstanding reggae acts quickly agreed to perform in the cause of peace. This was the apex of what most reggae observers agree was the music's finest hour: the roots era of the mid to late seventies. In the wake of Bob Marley's international success and self-imposed exile, hundreds of up-and-coming Jamaican artists were making outstanding music, and groups like Culture, the Mighty Diamonds, Wailing Souls, Inner Circle, and the Itals were filling the void that Bob had left. A new, dreader than dread crop of DJs, spearheaded by Big Youth, I-Roy, Trinity, and Dillinger, were also changing the direction of Jamaican music, bringing an even heavier sound, propelled by an ever more thunderous bass and extravagant stage personas.

Many of these acts agreed to donate their services to the cause of peace, and the organizers were able to guarantee a massive turnout by keeping ticket prices almost absurdly low: JA$2 for the Togetherness section, $5 for the Love section, and $8 for the best seats in the house, the Peace section. All proceeds were to go to the Peace Movement, and the poster advertising the concert was dominated by a picture of Haile Selassie I in Jamaica twelve years earlier.

In New York, meanwhile, Charles Comer was busy as always. The Peace Concert, by now, was a collective effort by Jamaica's reggae community to lend their hugely influential voices to the cause of peace; Comer presented the event to the media in a somewhat different light: it was, he told them, a Bob Marley concert, with a handful of opening acts thrown in to keep the crowd amused until the headliner hit the stage. Comer saw a once-in-a-lifetime opportunity to kick Bob's already successful career into the stratosphere, and he wasn't going to pass up on it. Soon he had a high-powered line-up of music writers committed to flying down to Kingston for the event, all on Island Records' dime. Island would pay for their plane tickets and their accommodation; all they had to take care of was their food and drink and whatever personal expenses they chose to incur. It was an offer they couldn't refuse, and within a few days of the announcement that it would be taking place the Peace Concert was guaranteed huge international media coverage.

Excitement mounted in Jamaica in the week leading up to the big show. And the violence, the raison d'être for the event, continued unchecked. Murder and mayhem competed with the Peace Concert for space in the *Gleaner* and *Observer* newspapers. Kingston was a seething cauldron of good versus evil, and once again Bob Marley was in the midst of it. Once again, his guitar was going to be his machine gun.

At 56 Hope Road, the runnings were remarkably cool. And so, as always, was Bob Marley, happy to be back on his home turf, happy to be with his own people, and as casual and unassuming as ever, despite his by now unquestioned status as the hottest star in the world of popular music.

One journalist, in Jamaica to cover the concert, recalls venturing into 56 Hope Road looking for Valerie Cowan, the irrepressible behind-the-scenes reggae organizer, promoter, and booster, and, in tandem with her then husband Tommy Cowan, the head of Talent Corporation, whose yard at 1c Oxford Road, just round the corner from the Pegasus hotel, was the hangout of choice for just about all the foremost musicians in the great roots era. The journalist spotted a gathering of dreadlocked Rastas, squatting and sitting in a circle under the imposing front portico of the elegant wooden mansion, working on their spliffs and engrossed in vigorous reasoning. He asked them if Valerie was anywhere around. One of the group, who'd had his back to the journalist, quickly rose to his feet and told the visitor: "Sure, mon, follow me." It quickly dawned on the writer that the man he was following was Bob Marley. He was too surprised to even beg for an interview. Marley led the visitor round the corner and into the main office of 56 Hope Road, which had been commandeered by Valerie Cowan as the Peace Concert's operational HQ. "Dis mon 'ere fe see you," Marley told Valerie, acknowledging the journalist's thanks with a courteous nod and wandering back to rejoin his bredren.

Such was the hype leading up to the Peace Concert, it could easily have been anti-climatic. As it turned out, it was everything the build-up had promised—and much, much, more.

The concert had been advertised to start at five o'clock, and, to the collective astonishment of the couple of thousand people scattered around the sprawling National Stadium at that hour, it started at five o'clock. The Peace Concert has been immortalized, and rightly so, for many reasons—the fact that it may have been the only reggae concert in history to start on time has seldom been one of them.

It was still daylight when Lloyd Parkes and We the People played the first notes of the Peace Concert and the hit-making young vocal trio the Meditations took the stage. They were followed by Althea and Donna, singing their No. 1 international hit "Uptown Top Ranking"; the powerful dub poet Oku Onouru; and, with the crowd growing and the sun by now giving way to a brilliant full moon, the livewire DJ Dillinger, the first performer of the evening to get more than a lukewarm response from the notoriously hard-to-please Jamaican audience.

Junior Tucker delivered a best-forgotten couple of numbers, followed by some inspired roots by Joseph Hill and Culture, whose "Two Sevens Clash" was the hottest single to hit Jamaica the previous year, an oh-so-young Dennis Brown, Big Youth, Trinity, the Mighty Diamonds, Inner Circle, fronted by the charismatic Jacob Miller, and a promising young singer called Beres Hammond, best known in those days as the lead vocalist of Zap Pow, a horn-driven and distinctly jazzy reggae band.

Among the audience that night were Rolling Stones lead singer Mick Jagger, a long-time reggae fan, who spent most of the show backstage with the ebullient Charles Comer, and, sitting next to Bob's mother Cedella, a pregnant Cindy Breakspeare—Bob's son Damian "Junior Gong" Marley wasn't to arrive on the scene for another three months.

Scores of journalists from around the world were also in the crowd, many of them puzzled at having been moved, a few minutes before the show started, from their designated press seats, about twenty rows back, to the very front row, a few feet from the stage and in front of Prime Minister Michael Manley and his entourage of cabinet ministers and VIPs, who were sitting in the second row to the right of the stage. To the left, opposition leader Edward Seaga and his cohorts were also in the second row and behind the press. Why, the visiting journalists wondered, had members of the not always popular foreign press been moved from their perfectly acceptable positions to the seats in front of Manley and Seaga? In protocol-conscious Jamaica it was an almost bizarre situation. Then it dawned on them: there were hundreds of heavily armed soldiers and police in the National Stadium, many of them extremely edgy and at least a dozen positioned directly under the stage. If, by any chance, the violence that had been plaguing Kingston for months was to spill over into the stadium that night and bullets were to start flying, the foreign press would effectively be acting as shields for the politicians. It wasn't a situation that made them feel particularly comfortable—and later that night, when Peter Tosh was in the midst of three incendiary speeches he delivered during his performance, with the politicians sitting grim-faced and thousands of ordinary

Jamaicans howling their support, they wondered if they might find themselves in the midst of a story they hadn't bargained on covering.

At one point it seemed—at least to those in those high-profile and high-risk seats—that Peter was deliberately inciting the crowd to riot, and they sat nervously wondering where the nearest exits were and if they'd be able to duck quickly enough if things did turn ugly. Fortunately, the lid stayed on.

Ras Michael and the Sons of Negus, who followed Peter, were considerably more soothing. Accompanied by white-robed dancers, the deeply spiritual singer-songwriter/master hand-drummer and this wonderful band transformed the by-now crammed National Stadium into what amounted to a gigantic Rastafarian grounation, and by the time the Sons of Negus left the stage the vibes were considerably less tense.

There was a lengthy break after Ras Michael, and anticipation mounted as instruments were set up for the Wailers. Almost casually, members of the band began to wander onto the stage, picking up their instruments and starting to play. It seemed more like a sound check than the headline act at a huge concert. It was now well after midnight, with the full moon and occasional flashes of lightning illuminating the crowd, and thunder booming in the distance. Everyone was waiting for Bob Marley to make a dramatic stage entrance. He didn't. The Wailers had by now settled into a gentle Rasta groove, and after a few minutes a disembodied, almost fragile-sounding voice, unmistakably Bob's, began to sing: "The Lion of Judah shall break every chain, the conquering lion, again and again." Then, from the right side of the stage, Bob Marley walked, ever so slowly, into history.

Soon the Wailers were in a heavier mood—they were playing the sort of reggae they knew Jamaicans wanted to hear. It was less rocky, less flashy, than when they were on tour, with Family Man and Carly, the Wailers roots, dictating the tempo and the mood. The tempo they chose was solid, bass- and drum-driven, and they soon had the other players of instruments—Chinna on rhythm guitar, Junior Marvin on lead, Tyrone and Wya on keyboards, Seeco on percussion, and a raunchy horn section of Glen DaCosta,

"Deadly" Headley Bennett, David Madden, and Vin Gordon—locked into a chugging, rock-solid, roots groove. To the right of the stage the I-Three added their sweet harmonies to the mix, skanking gracefully and resplendent in freshly minted Peace Concert T-shirts with Bob's image on the front (they were produced in several different colors but, to the frustration of thousands of would-be buyers, only one size: small).

Bob Marley's choice of songs that evening was inspired. "Conquering Lion" moved seamlessly into "Natural Mystic," and everyone in the stadium knew they were, indeed, in the presence of a natural mystic, and that he was part of them just as they were part of him. Then came a number just about everyone in the audience could identify with: "Trench Town Rock." By now the National Stadium was, without doubt, rocking. "Natty Dread" followed, then "Positive Vibration" and "War." It was becoming clear to everyone in the stadium that this was more than a mere concert: it was history in the making, and they were part of it.

What followed was, indeed, history—and the highest of drama. With thunder still echoing ominously, Bob and the band followed "War" with an inspired version of "Jamming," and the crowd started to sense that something unusual was about to happen. Still in their second-row seats, Michael Manley and Edward Seaga clearly had no clue that they were going to be part of it.

By now, Bob seemed to be defying gravity as he sang and danced. Still superbly fit, despite the problems with his foot, he launched himself into the air, arms akimbo, at the very second a colossal roll of thunder echoed around the stadium. It was an unforgettable moment: two mighty, mystical powers, orchestrated by who knows what, coming together in a single, transcendental instant. And the drama was just starting. Seconds later, Bob started scat-singing an invitation to the political leaders. His voice rising almost to a shriek, he exhorted them to join him on stage, to show the people in the National Stadium that they, too, wanted peace for Jamaica.

"To make everything come true, we've got to be together, yeah, yeah . . . To show the people that you love them right, to show the people that you're gonna unite, show the people that you're over bright, show the people that everything is all right. Watch, watch, watch, watch, watch, watch what you're doin'. I'm gonna send a message right out there. I'm not so good at talking but I hope you understand what I'm trying to say, well I'm trying to say, could we have, could we have, up here onstage here the presence of Mr. Michael Manley and Mr. Edward Seaga. I just want to shake hands and show the people that we're gonna make it right, we're gonna unite, we're gonna make it right . . . The moon is high over my head, and I give my love instead. The moon was high above my head, and yes I give my love instead."

For what seemed like an eternity neither Manley nor Seaga budged. It looked as though they had no intention of getting together on stage, in front of tens of thousands of people, and committing themselves to ending the tribal war that was threatening to engulf Jamaica. But mere politicians couldn't stand up to the compelling, majestic, magnetic force of Nesta Robert Marley. Seaga was the first to make a move, and he was quickly pulled to the stage. A few seconds later, Manley had no choice but to follow. By now, the stage was crowded, and many of those on it, weaving their way among the musicians and the island's two most powerful politicians, were ghetto gunmen and warlords who'd been watching from vantage points to the side. The Wailers—the most rigorously rehearsed band on the planet—hadn't missed a beat while all this was going on around them, and they still didn't as Marley took Manley's and Seaga's right hands, raised their arms, and joined them above his head. He kept them there for a few seconds, with the arch-rivals smiling somewhat uncomfortably— they'd almost certainly have preferred to throttle each other.

Then, almost before the audience realized it, Manley and Seaga were back in their seats and Bob was singing the theme song for the evening, "One Love," with a clearly uninhibited young boy, who'd been allowed to stay up way, way past his bedtime for the occasion, dancing onto the stage to join him. It was Ziggy Marley's first big show, and he was enjoying every second of it.

Then it was time for one last number—again a song chosen to capture the spirit of that momentous evening: "Jah Live."

Give peace a chance: Bob raises the hands of Prime Minister Michael Manley (left) and opposition leader Edward Seaga as they join him on stage during the historic One Love Concert for Peace in Kingston, 1978.

Then it was time to go home and hope that the Peace Concert wouldn't be in vain. Sadly, it was. The shooting and the mayhem would soon resume in Jamaica, and the elections that were to follow less than two years later were to be the most violent in the country's history.

Bucky Marshall and Claudie Massop were both to meet violent deaths not long after their unsuccessful attempt to bring peace to Jamaica. Marshall was shot and killed at a Jamaican dance in Brooklyn, New York, in 1980. Massop was stopped by police at a road block in Kingston in 1979 and shot to death. The cops said he was armed and it was a shootout. An enterprising photographer for the tabloid *Observer* managed to sneak into the mortuary where Massop's bullet-riddled body—he'd stopped forty-four shots—was lying on a slab. The graphic picture showed at least half a dozen bullet wounds under Massop's right armpit, the most unlikely part of the anatomy to stop a bullet . . . unless the victim's arms happen to be raised above his head.

A final less than peaceful Peace Concert footnote: the day after the concert, two visiting journalists dropped by the Intercontinental hotel, near Kingston's waterfront, on their way to the airport to fly back to North America. They were there to say their goodbyes to Charles Comer. As they walked into the hotel, they were confronted by the sight of the powerful Liverpudlian pinning a squirming and helpless man against a pillar in the middle of the lobby with his right hand, and slapping him on the face repeatedly with his left. Between each slap, he was delivering a loud, profanity-riddled lecture:

> Don't you ever
>
> *Slap*
>
> Try that kind
>
> *Slap*
>
> Of fuckin' thing
>
> *Slap*
>
> With me
>
> *Slap*
>
> Again
>
> *Slap*
>
> If you know
>
> *Slap*
>
> What's fuckin'
>
> *Slap*
>
> Good for you.

As everyone in the lobby watched in astonishment, Comer finally let go of his victim, who slunk away without a word.

Then Comer spotted his friends and greeted them with a cheery hello. "What on earth was that all about, Charlie?" one of them asked.

"The bastard deserved worse," snorted Comer. "He's a writer and we paid his air fare and hotel and I just found out he'd put all his food and drinks on my tab. He won't try that again, heh, heh, heh."

Comer was to work for Bob for another year or so, then switched camps, joining Peter Tosh and, as always, devoting himself unstintingly to launching a non-stop media blitz and doing Peter's career inestimable good. It was Comer who orchestrated Peter's famous duet with Mick Jagger on *Saturday Night Live*. He was also one of the few human beings capable of intimidating the proud and sometimes short-fused Tosh. Peter would meekly acquiesce to anything Comer demanded, even to the extent of putting out a barely lit morning spliff when the PR guru brusquely told him he was running late for an important interview and ordered him to get a move on.

Charles Comer died in the early winter of 1999. He played a significant role in the careers of both Bob Marley and Peter Tosh, a contribution to their success that has been largely unacknowledged—which is exactly how the quintessential behind-the-scenes PR man would have wanted it.

15.
The Price of Fame

The Peace Concert was barely over when it was time, once again, for the movement of Jah people. Bob's foot seemed to be on the mend—Marley bredren said they'd never seen him move the way he did at the National Stadium during the dramatic performance of "Jamming"—and, after the necessary but disappointing cancellation of the North American part of the *Exodus* tour, the Wailers were keen to get back on the road in support of another new album, *Kaya*.

The album's reception had been somewhat lukewarm. As always the press was ready to pounce, and the prevailing wisdom, at least in media circles, was that Bob Marley had "gone soft." Even though it had been recorded at the same sessions as *Exodus*, *Kaya* had none of the fire and brimstone of the first side of that epic album, nor, even, of the albums that had preceded it. It was more tranquil, less rebellious, and the mainstream press, most of whom hadn't caught up with Bob's career until *Rastaman Vibration* and *Exodus*, were quick to criticize. The vast majority of the hypercritical scribes were totally unaware that Bob's career had already taken many musical twists and turns, that over the years he'd recorded everything from love songs dripping with teenage angst to more-than-passable doo-wop to frenzied James Brown covers. All they knew was that Jamaica's soul rebel was in a different space with *Kaya*, and they seized on the opportunity to pour scorn. Eventually, *Kaya* would come to be appreciated for what it was and is: another Bob Marley and the Wailers masterwork.

The cover alone was worth the price of admission: perhaps the greatest of the many wonderful pictures Kate Simon took of Bob. The music was rather special too, a mixture of the pastoral and the downright bright and breezy. And, despite what the critics had to say, it was anything but lightweight. Among the tracks was one of Bob's most under-appreciated songs about the human condition in general, "Running Away." Sung largely in a jazzy, almost conversational semi-growl, it's a song that admonishes listeners to look inside themselves: "You're running and you're running and you're running away, but you can't run away from yourself, can't run away from yourself."

The Wailers party that flew from Kingston to the United States in May 1978 for the start of the *Kaya* tour was the line-up that remained the nucleus of the band for the rest of Bob's life. Al Anderson had been welcomed back into the group after about a year touring and recording with Peter Tosh (his replacement in Peter's band, in what had become almost a reggae game of musical guitars, was Donald Kinsey). The combination of Al and Junior Marvin gave the Wailers a formidable duo of lead guitars. With a sound grounded by the rootsmen in the group, Fams, Carly, Tyrone, Wya, and Seeco, and with a full complement of I-Three providing soulful harmonies, this was, without apology, without a semblance of doubt, the tightest, toughest, finest band in the world.

The hectic tour took the triumphant Wailers back and forth across the Atlantic. After more than twenty US and Canadian dates in less than a month—in the midst of which Bob was awarded a United Nations Medal of Peace "on behalf of 500 million Africans" in a ceremony at New York's Waldorf-Astoria hotel—they performed in England, France, Spain, Sweden, Denmark, Norway, Holland, and Belgium, with particularly memorable shows in Amsterdam, Paris, Copenhagen, and London's Lyceum that were immortalized in the following year's double live album, *Babylon by Bus*. After the European leg of the tour the Wailers returned to the United States, and only three days after their Lyceum show they were on the west coast at the Burbank Starlight Bowl in L.A. As always when the Wailers played in the world capital of showbiz, there was a star-studded audience, among them the Rolling Stones' Mick Jagger. But the show was historic for another, much more significant, reason: also in the audience was Peter Tosh, whose tour schedule happened to have him in L.A. at the same time as the Wailers. And when Bob launched into "Get Up Stand Up" near the end of the set, Peter bounded onto the stage, grabbed the mike, and, as the delighted Marley broke into a high-steppin' dance, the clock was turned back for a few precious moments, with the two original Wailers reunited in a song they'd written together all those years ago. Neither was to know, as their voices soared in righteous unison, their spot-on harmonizing a testimonial to the patient coaching of Professor Joe Higgs, that it was the last time they'd be on a stage together this side of Zion.

The tour wound up in Miami in August, and Bob took the welcome opportunity to spend some time with his mother, Cedella. On his return to Jamaica he could hardly wait to start recording again. By now he'd realized his cherished ambition of owning a studio of his own. It was called, appropriately enough, Tuff Gong, it was state of the art, and it was located on the ground floor of the world headquarters of reggae music, 56 Hope Road.

Early in 1979, work began at Tuff Gong on an album that was to be called *Survival*, and which many Marley fans insist to this day is the best of them all. That's open to debate, but what isn't in any doubt is that *Survival* was and is a superlative album. It is permeated with African themes, and it's probably no accident that the first track to be recorded and released from a session at the brand-new studio, with the Tuff Gong himself at the controls, set the tone for the rest of the sessions: it was called "Africa Unite."

The tracks that followed were equally compelling: "One Drop," "Zimbabwe"—soon to become that fledgling nation's unofficial national anthem—"Survival," "Babylon System," "Ride Natty Ride," "So Much Trouble," "Top Rankin'," "Wake up and Live," and "Ambush in the Night," the song inspired by the 1976 shooting nightmare at 56 Hope Road, rounded out an album that was majestic even by Bob Marley's standards.

No sooner were the final tracks of *Survival* completed than the Wailers were once again on the road, and this time the road took them to places they'd never ventured before—Japan, New

Zealand, Australia, and Hawaii. Again, the tour was a triumph. Japan, in particular, was a hotbed of reggae, and the arrival of the Wailers in early April 1979 was a monumental occasion for the nation's legion of Marley fans. The concert promoters, having heard of the band's copious appetite for herb, went out of their way to gather in what they thought would be enough to last them for the week of the tour—and were nonplussed when the Wailers, entirely predictably, smoked it all on their first day in the country. More was procured, and the tour continued happily, with six shows in Tokyo and two in Osaka.

From Japan the Wailers flew to New Zealand, where they performed in Auckland, after which they headed to Australia for shows in Brisbane, Adelaide, Perth, Melbourne, and Sydney. On the way home to Jamaica, the Wailers stopped for a few days in Hawaii in early May, where they played in Maui and Oahu and enthusiastically sampled the delights of the legendary Hawaiian Gold herb.

By now Bob Marley was successful to a degree he could barely have imagined a few years earlier. He'd started the seventies penniless, hungry, and homeless. As the decade drew to its close, he was a multi-millionaire, the Third World's first superstar, worshipped by millions of reggae fans throughout the world, a virtual god to millions in Africa. But not all the changes in his life were for the better. He had become so famous, so much in demand, that he rarely had a minute of peace, a moment to himself. Fame has its price, and for Bob, always generous and giving with his time, it was a steep one. There must have been times he longed to be back in Nine Mile, hanging, reasoning, and licking the chalice with his undemanding country friends and family.

Following the hugely successful Asian dates, the Wailers were due for a few months' break home in Jamaica before resuming the *Survival* tour in the United States and Canada in October. They also had an important concert date in Jamaica. Bob had been asked to headline Reggae Sunsplash, a new festival that aspired to be the world's biggest annual showcase for reggae music. Sunsplash had made its debut the previous year at Jarrett Park, a cricket and soccer stadium in the heart of Montego Bay, the hustling, bustling tourist mecca on Jamaica's north coast. The first event had been a big success, culturally if not commercially (the crowds were ample, but many of them had simply climbed the walls surrounding the venue), and the Sunsplash organizers—four reggae-crazy young Jamaican businessmen, Tony Johnson, Ronnie Burke, John Wakeling, and Don Greene—wanted the country's biggest star to give them the sort of boost they needed to take it to the next level. Always ready to help fellow Jamaicans, Bob agreed to perform.

His 7 July appearance at Sunsplash was memorable for many reasons. For one thing, it had been raining in Montego Bay—long, hard, and heavy. The festival was to go down in history as Reggae Mudsplash, and the thousands who jammed into Jarrett Park for Bob's eagerly awaited appearance found themselves ankle-deep in mud. For another, Bob gave an epic performance, playing the sort of rootical reggae he reserved for Jamaica. What made the occasion truly historic, although no one knew it at the time, was that it was the last time he would perform live in the land of his birth. The last song Bob Marley was ever to sing before an audience in Jamaica was the one he chose to close his encore: "Exodus."

There were only the smallest of clues that Bob Marley was a dying man, that the cancer that he thought had been cured was starting to spread through his wiry frame. He was as dynamic as ever on stage and he was back to playing soccer with his customary enthusiasm and skill. But he was starting to look a little gaunt, and he seemed, somehow, to be not quite his old self. There wasn't as much laughter any more, and he was just a little sharper with those around him than he used to be.

The constant demands now being made on his time didn't help. Bob never embraced the superstar lifestyle—at the pinnacle of his success, he was as humble, as accessible, as down to earth as he'd been in the days when he was sleeping rough in Trench Town. But it sometimes seemed that everyone wanted a slice of him, and usually they got it. Bob's unfailing generosity, be it with his time or with his money, made him vulnerable to all the demands. Years after his passing, Cindy Breakspeare was asked if she felt the constant clamor for Bob's attention had played a role in his early death. Her response was unequivocal: "Oh yes. He never ever turned people away. Never. He was just so pressured by people everywhere he went . . . they were just drawn like moths to a flame, they couldn't stay away."

Later in July, Bob accepted an invitation to play at another major event—this time in Boston, a reggae-loving city that had welcomed him warmly and appreciatively many times in the past. The occasion was a special one. The concert he'd agreed to appear in was a benefit for a cause always close to his heart: the proceeds were to go to the African National Congress and other liberation forces in southern Africa. Bob said he'd play for $10,000, and the concert, at which he was introduced by comedian and social activist Dick Gregory, is widely regarded as one of the greatest of his career. It was unusual in that he even delivered a speech, something he almost never did, maintaining that he said everything he had to say in his songs, and that if people didn't get the message from them they weren't about to get it anyway. In the course of the speech, the mesmerized audience were the first people to hear the words many regard as Bob Marley's greatest, and which were to be the basis for the still-to-be-written "Redemption Song": "Emancipate yourself from mental slavery; none but ourselves can free our minds."

The Amandla concert also gave Bob an indication that the days of being ripped off weren't necessarily consigned to history. He was asked by an interviewer why he'd charged $20,000 to play at a benefit for African freedom fighters. Don Taylor, it turned out, had upped the fee, unknown to Bob. It's not known what happened to the extra $10,000, but the incident added to Bob's nagging suspicions about the honesty of his hustling, jive-talking manager.

After the Amandla concert Bob Marley had a brief respite from the rigors of touring, and spent some of the time relaxing with his mother at her new home in Miami. During that period, Cedella recalls, there was an ominous incident with Taylor. Bob, she says, "backed up Don Taylor in the drawing room and gave him a good thump, toppling him over on his backside."

The problems between Bob and Don Taylor were to come to a head a few months later, in the African nation of Gabon, but first the Wailers had to undertake yet another major tour, again in support of *Survival*. It started in late October with seven shows in the fabled Apollo Theater, on 125th Street in the heart of New York's Harlem. The theater, which opened in 1913 as a whites-only burlesque hall in the days when America was heavily segregated, became a shrine of black culture in the mid-thirties, and its hallowed stage had seen performances by virtually every African-American star, among them Aretha Franklin, Ella Fitzgerald, Count Basie, Duke Ellington, Nat King Cole, Sammy Davis Jr, Stevie Wonder, Sarah Vaughan, Josephine Baker, Sam Cooke, Marvin Gaye, James Brown, B. B. King, Bessie Smith, Mahalia Jackson, Louis Armstrong, Al Green, Diana Ross and the Supremes, Gladys Knight and the Pips, and Billie Holiday. Bob Marley had long been frustrated by the resistance of African Americans to reggae, and although he could easily have filled a much bigger venue he was determined to take his music and his message of Rastafari to the temple of black American culture.

Despite suffering from a hard-to-shake cold—his overall health wasn't getting any better—Bob's Apollo performances were riveting. The Apollo run opened on 25 October 1979, with the staccato organ chords and throbbing bass that announced to the crowd packed into the historic theater that a new, different black superstar was among them, a true Natural Mystic.

The tour continued at breakneck pace with a swing into Canada immediately after the Apollo shows, and by the time the Wailers were heading back to Jamaica in December, Bob Marley had played more than forty concerts in something like a month and a half, many of them in northern cities where the weather was cold and dismal. The reviews were glowing, and the tour boosted the sales of the *Survival* album, but it wasn't terribly beneficial for Bob's deteriorating health.

The Wailers had barely arrived in Jamaica when it was time to leave the island once again—this time for another date with history, their first performance in Africa. They'd been invited to make a special appearance at the birthday celebrations for Gabon's president, Omar Bongo, on 4 January 1980, and the invitation had come from the African ruler's daughters, with whom Bob had become friendly—very friendly, according to some sources—in Los Angeles during the *Survival* tour. The Wailers were disappointed when they discovered that the show for which they'd made the long and arduous journey was a private affair, for the West African nation's elite, and Bob was downright furious when he discovered, almost inadvertently, that the fee for the show was $60,000. Bob had told Don Taylor that the band would play for $40,000, a large chunk of which had been eaten up in their traveling expenses; he was livid when he realized his fast-talking manager had pocketed the extra $20,000 . . . and he knew it almost certainly wasn't the first time he'd been ripped off by the man he'd trusted to take care of business.

Bob confronted Taylor, and while the story of what happened next varies, depending largely on the recollections of the people who were there, what is known is that the Trench Town toughness of Bob Marley surfaced and he gave the sobbing Taylor a sound thrashing.

Years later, two members of the I-Three were to recall what happened in Gabon.

Judy Mowatt said: "Bob tried to keep it as covered up as he could, but we knew what was going on. Don got a licking and a kicking from Bob that day, for stealing money."

Rita Marley was even more specific: "That was an exposure, the pinnacle of all that Don had been doing over the years. Bob was the kind of man who doesn't really look into documents and contracts. So Don was having a ball. He was making big bucks... He was very dangerous."

Said Bob himself: "Don too tricky, yunno . . . Is better that somebody ask you for something and get it more, than try trick me fe mek it. I'm no fool."

Not long after the Gabon incident Don Taylor was fired, and before long it was business as usual for the Wailers—they were back in the Tuff Gong studio, laying down the tracks for what would be the last album Bob Marley was to see released in his life-time. Uprising was another master work, from beginning—"Coming in From the Cold," with a distinctly African, highly percussive guitar intro by Junior Marvin—to end—a stunning, acoustic version of a number many regarded as the songwriting apex of Bob Marley's career, "Redemption Song."

While *Uprising* was being recorded, Bob Marley received another invitation to perform in Africa—this time an event of considerably more significance than a birthday party. The government of Zimbabwe wanted him to play at the nation's upcoming independence ceremonies. They wanted the man whose stirring anthem—"Africans a liberate Zimbabwe"—had inspired their freedom fighters in the late stages of their guerrilla war. They wanted him to be there when the Union Jack was lowered. They wanted the man who had reassured them, in song, "brother you're right, you're right, you're so right" to be there when prophecy was fulfilled.

The only problem was that they couldn't afford to pay for all the Wailers, so they wanted Bob alone. His response was typical: he wouldn't perform without his band, and he'd foot the bills himself. By now, despite the rip-offs and the vast amounts of money he'd given away, Bob Marley was a rich man—and on what better to spend his money than being part of the birth of a new African nation?

In April 1980 the plane carrying the Wailers' equipment touched down in Salisbury, the capital of what was still Rhodesia. Bob and the band were to arrive a few days later on a regular commercial flight. After the airport formalities—most of the new government's cabinet ministers were there to greet them—the Wailers soon found themselves gravitating towards the people they felt most comfortable with: the freedom fighters who had been inspired by their music. And they were profoundly touched when the guerrillas told them they had listened to Wailers music—and particularly "Zimbabwe"—constantly when they were in the field, risking their lives for their nation's freedom.

The independence ceremonies were held on 18 April in the Rufaro Stadium, about ten miles outside of Salisbury. The plan—

for want of a better word—was for the crowd to be limited to officially invited guests (among them Britain's Prince Charles and Indian Prime Minister Indira Gandhi). But this was Africa, and there was no way Bob Marley was going to play for Zimbabwe's independence without the people of the new nation being part of the occasion. When the Union Jack had been lowered, and the Wailers had started their set with "Natural Mystic," the gates to the stadium were broken down by the pressure of those locked outside. Tens of thousands of excited citizens rushed in as the set continued with "Positive Vibration," "Roots Rock Reggae," and "Lively Up Yourself." Then came the song everyone had been waiting to hear: "Zimbabwe." But the situation inside the stadium quickly became so volatile that security forces panicked and unleashed tear gas to try to control the crowd, and it started to drift towards the musicians. Rita, Marcia, and Judy fled the stage, and so eventually did the male Wailers. Before long, Bob, who had continued singing in a world of his own, realized what was going on. He finished "Zimbabwe," and remarked famously to the I-Three when he saw them backstage a few moments later, "Now we know who the real revolutionaries are!"

Such was the chaos that the Wailers decided to do another show the next night, this time with no partiality: it was to be for the people of Zimbabwe. An estimated 100,000 crowded into the Rufaro Stadium the following evening, and the Wailers performed for about an hour and a half. But Bob wasn't at his best. Some surmised that the events of the previous evening had taken their toll; perhaps, but his own deteriorating health couldn't have helped.

Two or three days later, with the band back in London, the Wailers were pictured by Adrian Boot, one of the foremost photographic chroniclers of Bob's career, in an elevator of the London hotel in which they were staying. Bob Marley looked haggard and drawn, almost ominously so, in the first group shot of the Wailers since the days of *Catch a Fire*.

The two things Bob Marley needed most at this stage of his life were some proper medical attention and a long rest, a break from the rollercoaster of success and its incessant demands. Instead, the month after the Zimbabwe concerts, he and the Wailers were back in Jamaica to do more recording—the tracks they laid down included "Buffalo Soldier," "Jump Nyabinghi," "Chant Down Babylon," "Trench Town," and "Stiff Necked Fools." "Buffalo Soldier" and "Trench Town" were released as singles; the other tracks wouldn't be heard by the world until almost two years after Bob's passing, on the posthumous album *Confrontation*.

And in late May they found themselves once more at Norman Manley International Airport, boarding a jet to Europe for a huge tour to support the newly released *Uprising* album. As their plane took off and began its leisurely climb over the blue waters of the Caribbean, with the majestic Blue Mountains fading in the distance to the left, it seemed like the start of a routine Atlantic crossing, very much business as usual in the Wailers' hectic lives. Bob Marley had no way of knowing it would be the last time he would see Jamaica.

The *Uprising* tour started in Zurich, Switzerland, and continued triumphantly through Germany, France, Norway, Sweden, Denmark, Belgium, Holland, Italy, Spain, Ireland, England, and Scotland. In Italy the Wailers played for more than 100,000 people at Milan's cavernous San Siro Stadium, home of that city's two legendary soccer clubs, AC Milan and Inter-Milan. It was an attendance record that stands to this day—and Bob must have taken a certain degree of malicious satisfaction from the fact that he had easily outdrawn Pope John Paul II, who had appeared there a few days before (John Paul was the incumbent in an office detested by Rastafarians since an earlier pope had blessed Mussolini's warplanes as they were about to take off to bomb Ethiopia in the late thirties).

After Europe, the Wailers crossed the Atlantic to continue the *Uprising* tour in the United States, but first Bob took a break in Miami, to spend some time with his mother and gather his strength for the demanding concerts ahead of him. By now, he was clearly a very sick man, and Al Anderson, visiting him in Miami, recalls Bob telling him, "I got a pain in my throat and my head, and it's killing me."

The US leg of the *Uprising* tour was scheduled to kick off in

Boston, and the Wailers played one show there in mid-September and another in Providence, Rhode Island, before heading for New York, where they were booked for two concerts at Madison Square Garden. Bob, still eager to reach a black American audience, had agreed to equal billing on those shows with the immensely popular Commodores, with the Wailers the opening act.

Bob's health was visibly deteriorating, and so were the vibes surrounding the tour. Like piranhas, a bunch of shady hustlers were crowding Bob Marley; it was a vastly different scene from the tightly knit group of righteous Rastas of earlier tours, and in New York Bob was even booked into a separate hotel from the band. He stayed at the usual Wailers New York base, the Essex House, while the band members, to their chagrin, were checked into the Gramercy Park, about forty blocks away.

The scene at the Essex House was an ugly one, with Bob's suite besieged by a variety of hustlers and criminal types, among them, by all accounts, Vivian Blake, a charismatic, well-educated, and ruthless Jamaican drug kingpin in New York, and one of his accomplices, known only as Baskin. Blake was soon to became one of the founders and leaders of the murderous Shower Posse, perhaps the most feared criminal organization in the history of the United States.

Despite his failing health, Bob Marley was still eager to keep as fit as he could, and on 21 September, the day after the second show at Madison Square Garden, he decided to go for a run in Central Park with Skill Cole, by now back in the Wailers' fold, and a few other members of the Wailers' entourage. As he was jogging, Bob collapsed. He had suffered some sort of seizure, and although he never lost consciousness he was clearly scared.

Traveling with the Wailers was one of the few doctors Bob Marley trusted, Carl "Pee Wee" Frazier. A fellow Jamaican, he had been part of the Wailers' inner circle for years, and he quickly arranged for Bob to visit a neurologist in New York. The Wailers flew to Pittsburgh, where their next concert was scheduled, and Bob told the band he'd join them later. But they were worried—and with good reason.

The news from the neurologist was brutal. The cancer Bob

thought he had beaten had spread through his body and had reached his brain. The pain in his head he had been complaining about to Al Anderson in Miami had been caused by a large brain tumor and it was, indeed, killing him. The doctor told him he might have only two to three weeks to live.

Bob Marley was shattered. He'd often told people that the only thing he had of real worth was his life, and that he wanted to use it to do as much good as possible for as many people as possible and to spread the message of Rastafari. Now, at the age of thirty-five, he'd been told that his life was soon going to end. There was only one thing he could do: catch a plane to Pittsburgh, play what might be his final concert, then seek further medical advice.

At the sound check in Pittsburgh's Stanley Theater on the afternoon of 23 September, Bob kept on repeating "Keep on Moving," a song that had deep significance for him and for the Barrett brothers: they'd first recorded it together at Randy's in Kingston in 1971, with Bunny and Peter singing behind Bob. And it was the song Bob had chosen to send a message to his family in Jamaica when he was in exile in London in 1977. This time he was singing it to say farewell to his Wailers.

For that night's concert, Bob gathered his failing strength, and the show was a memorable one. It began with "Natural Mystic," and for ninety minutes Bob Marley poured his heart and soul into his final live performance. It ended with an encore set that started with "Redemption Song," continuing with "Coming in From the Cold," "Could You Be Loved," "Is This Love," and finally a medley of "Work" and "Get Up Stand Up."

The rest of the tour was officially cancelled late that evening, and the world was told that Bob Marley was exhausted.

Further medical tests followed over the next few days, in Miami and New York, and they confirmed the worst: the cancer had reached Bob's brain and invaded the rest of his body. Radiation treatment was started in New York, and Bob Marley, who had probably been the fittest and most health-conscious star in the history of popular music, started to lose weight and to lose his locks. Bob was baptized, at the behest of his family, into the

Ethiopian Orthodox Church, and, with Rita and the children watching, christened Berhane Selassie: "Light of the Holy Trinity."

After much squabbling among his inner circle, with Bob—their unquestioned boss for so many years—reduced by his illness to the role of onlooker, it was eventually decided that his best chance of survival was to put himself in the hands of a controversial German doctor, viewed with enormous skepticism by many in the medical profession but with a reputation for success with cancer patients other doctors had given up on. Dr. Josef Issels had been an officer in Hitler's SS during the Second World War, and his clinic in the Bavarian Alps was in a place that was alien in every way to Bob Marley. Many around him, including Cindy Breakspeare, felt he'd have had a better chance of living if he'd been in a warm, familiar climate. "If it was left to me and me alone," she would tell an interviewer years later, "I would have said St. Ann. With lots of organically grown vegetables, tea, a good rest, and just deal with it a different way. I wouldn't really have added to the stress by placing him in a strange place in a climate he hated, surrounded by people he didn't know. I never agreed with that decision and I know Rita didn't either. But we didn't have much say. We were merely women. And the brethren seemed to think that Bavaria was the best place."

Bob was flown to Bavaria in November 1980, and put himself in the care of Josef Issels.

Bob's strength, both mental and physical, helped him to live for six more months, much longer than doctors in America had believed possible. But it was a sad and painful period, recalls his mother, Cedella, who was with him for much of the time, along with Skill Cole, Dr. Frazier, and a Jamaican acquaintance from Trench Town, known only as Bird, who was there as a cook and all-round helper. There were frequent visits—from members of the Wailers, from Cindy Breakspeare, from Pascalene Bongo, the daughter of the Gabon president, and from Chris Blackwell, who sadly recalls a deteriorating Bob Marley as looking "like a man of eighty."

Eventually, in early May 1981, Josef Issels gave up on Nesta Robert Marley. "He's not going to live," he told Cedella.

The following day, arrangements were made to take Bob back to Jamaica to die. A 747 jet was chartered to fly him first to Miami, where his wife and children awaited him, and Bob Marley, accompanied by his mother, long-time friends and confidantes Denise Mills and Diane Jobson, two doctors and a nurse, prepared for his final journey. At the airport, near death though he was, he still gave of himself, signing autographs for customs and immigration officials.

Ten hours later, on Saturday, 9 May, the jumbo jet touched down at Miami International Airport, and Bob was immediately taken to Cedars of Lebanon Hospital. He was put into intensive care, and the doctors there said all they could do was make him as comfortable as possible.

He wouldn't be able to go home to die; he simply wasn't strong enough to endure another flight.

The following day Bob was visited by Rita, accompanied by the younger and older Cedellas, his sons Ziggy and Stephen, and Richard, his mother's fifteen-year-old son from her marriage to Mr. Booker. Cindy Breakspeare and their son Damian, by now almost two years old, also visited Bob that day, and, despite his extreme weakness, he still managed to say to her slyly, "Hmmmph, think you never did a come."

The following morning, Monday, 11 May, Bob's mother returned to Cedars of Lebanon to visit her dying son. She gave him some carrot juice to drink and he told her, "I'm going to take a rest now."

Then Bob Marley closed his eyes and fell into a sleep he was never to awaken from.

A few minutes later Diane Jobson went into the room to check on her beloved friend. She quickly called for Cedella and told her Bob wasn't breathing. They summoned a nurse, who checked Bob's pulse, and said to them quietly: "He's deceased."

At that moment, Judy Mowatt was home in Jamaica. She didn't know that Bob Marley, the man she'd loved as a brother and had traveled the world with, had just passed away. Judy recalls: "It was broad daylight, and there was this great, huge thunder in the heavens. And a flash of lightning came through the house. It came through the window and lodged for about a second on Bob's picture. We didn't know at the time, the radio stations hadn't gotten the news officially to announce it, but people could know that something had happened and that the heavens were really responding to a great force being taken away from the physical plane of the earth."

16.

Home to Rest

Events of significance that took place on 21 May 1981.

• In Paris, François Mitterrand became president of France.

• In the Vatican, Pope John Paul II continued to recover from bullet wounds that had almost killed him in an assassination attempt eight days earlier.

• In Nine Mile, deep in the heart of rural Jamaica, Nesta Robert Marley was laid to rest.

The humble messenger of Rastafari was honored with a state funeral, and it was a funeral unlike any the Caribbean had seen. Tears flowed, but there was joy and music as well—strictly Wailers music—as his people said farewell to their beloved Bob Marley in true Jamaican style.

The formalities were minimal, fitting for a man who had no time for pomp and pride. There was a service at Kingston's National Arena, with Rasta drumming, an eloquent eulogy by Prime Minister Edward Seaga, and the I-Three pouring their souls into the familiar refrain from "Rastaman Chant," words that said everything that needed to be said, everything that could be said:

"Fly away home to Zion, fly away home,

One bright morning, when my work is over, I will fly away home."

Then they took Bob Marley home.

The coffin was placed on the back of a humble pickup truck, the daily transportation of necessity for working men throughout the Caribbean, and, with tens of thousands lining the route, Bob's last physical journey started. Led by dreadlocked Rastas on CB200s, the funeral procession retraced the route Bob Marley had taken on a country bus with his father thirty years earlier. Along the way, at a place called Cotton Tree, the blue pickup broke down, and there was a longish wait while emergency repairs were carried out.

Hours later, the procession reached Nine Mile, where thousands had gathered to await Bob Marley's final homecoming.

The hillsides the teenage Cedella Malcolm had negotiated so adroitly on the way to her late-night trysts with Norval Marley in 1944 were a sea of people. Bob's resting place, a white mausoleum, had been erected—Jamaican-style, with standard cinder blocks assembled by spliff-smoking, dreadlocked workers—a few feet from the tiny wooden house Omeriah Malcolm had built for Cedella and her young son, the home in which Bob had spent his happiest childhood years, the country roots to which he'd returned with Rita when the pressures of Kingston had become too much for him.

Judy Mowatt was in the funeral procession as it wound its way from Kingston to Nine Mile. "All of Jamaica turned out, from the babe on the breast to the schoolchildren, even the elderly, everybody came out. It was more like a jubilee, everybody had a nice time, music was playing, and the procession was going very fast. I was so glad I was able to bless my eyes on Bob's birthplace. I wasn't even able to see the mausoleum because of the huge crowd that was there. Even people who had not known him in his lifetime came out to see and pay their respects to him. It was like a jam session."

Bob's coffin was gently placed on a platform about three feet from the base of the mausoleum. In it with him were his guitar and his Bible. The mausoleum was sealed, first with a red metal plate, then with a steel grille, then with a layer of cement.

Bob Marley had done his earthly work. He'd carried the message of Rastafari to the far corners of the planet.

Already, he'd influenced and changed millions of lives, all for the better. In the decades ahead, his words and music were to do the same for countless millions more.

Now, he was home. It was time, finally, to rest.

17.
The Legacy

He may have been a prophet, but no one would have been more astonished than Bob Marley at much of what has happened since he left us, at least in the physical sense, on that sad day in May 1981.

Much of what has come to pass would have hurt and dismayed him. Without Bob to lead the way and keep those around him on a path of righteousness, Babylon has wormed its way into what he left behind, and into reggae music itself.

Much, though, would have pleased him. And what would have pleased him most is that his message of peace, brotherhood, tolerance, understanding, and one love has reached a universal audience he could barely have dreamed of when he was alive. His music has uplifted the existence of millions around the world, many of whom weren't born when Bob was with us. Today, countless people virtually live their lives by him, and many swear that Bob Marley is, single-handedly, responsible for making those lives worth living.

Bob's music continues to account for about half of all reggae sales, and his iconic image has become a symbol of recognition and brotherhood throughout the world. Simply wearing a Marley T-shirt, and there are hundreds, if not thousands, of different shirts bearing Bob's image, is a virtual guarantee of warm greetings from Moscow to Mombasa, from Rotterdam to Rio, from Beijing to Boston. Along the way, the teachings, values, and philosophies of Rastafari have become accepted and respected by people throughout the world. Bob would have loved that.

What he wouldn't have loved is the squabbling over the millions he left behind and the hundreds of millions his estate is now worth. As his music continues to sell in major-league quantities throughout the world, and his image is marketed in ways he could never have conceived (a Bob Marley luxury resort and spa in the Bahamas? A Bob Marley restaurant/nightclub named "Tribute to Freedom" at Disney World in Orlando?), seemingly interminable court battles have involved virtually everyone who was ever close to him. Among them: Rita Marley, most of his acknowledged children, Bunny Wailer, Danny Sims, Clement Dodd, Chris Blackwell, Aston Barrett, the other members of the Wailers band, and the estates of Peter Tosh and Carlton Barrett. And he wouldn't have been too pleased that lawyers have made a lot more money out of the music he made than the musicians who helped him make it.

The gold rush began almost as soon as Bob was laid to rest. A major problem, and more than a quarter century after his passing it continues to be one, is that one of the things Bob didn't leave behind was a will. In the absence of any clear statement of intent from Marley himself, his widow acted swiftly and decisively to ensure that what Bob had left behind came under her control.

But Rita was getting some bad advice, and her moves to consolidate the estate under what came to be known as the Rita Marley Group of Companies led to a legal nightmare that resulted, in 1986, in the Jamaica Supreme Court dismissing Rita as executor and passing the duties exclusively to the Mutual Security Merchant Bank and Trust Company, which had previously shared administrative duties—but not the cash—with Bob's widow.

Mutual Security promptly accused Rita and her advisers of diverting estate assets and royalties into their own bank accounts via international corporations. Rita was alleged to have forged Bob Marley's signature on documents that supposedly transferred some of his interests to her before he died, which would have meant they weren't part of the estate.

The result, bizarrely, was that the Marley estate was essentially put up for sale by Mutual to the highest bidder. Among the prospective buyers at one stage were the Japanese-controlled MCA record company; Eddy Grant, the shrewd Guyanese-born, Barbados-based entrepreneur/musician; and Island Logic, Chris Blackwell's New York-based holding company.

Eventually the Marley family and Blackwell came together and made a joint bid for the estate, and in December 1991 it was awarded to them by the Jamaica Supreme Court. The financial ramifications of the US$11.5 million bid remain cloudy to this day.

The following year, the drama moved to the Big Apple. A suit against Rita's attorney, David Steinberg, and her accountant, Marvin Zolt—both of whom had worked for Bob when he was alive and were intimately familiar with the intricacies of his financial empire—had been filed in 1986 by Mutual Security. Rita was not named as a defendant at the time, but was subsequently named as a third-party defendant.

By the time the suit finally went before a Federal District Court jury in New York in 1992, the plaintiff had been changed from Mutual Security to J. Reid Bingham, who had been appointed ancillary administrator of the estate in that jurisdiction. Steinberg and Zolt were accused of violations under the US anti-racketeering act, fraud, breach of fiduciary duty, negligence, and gross negligence for improperly diverting the estate's assets.

The estate originally alleged—and submitted an accounting report to back up their contention—that $13.4 million had been diverted from the estate between 1981 and 1986 ($2.9 million in bank accounts that had existed when Bob died, a further $10.5 million in royalties since his death). After taking into account funds diverted and recovered by the estate and payments that had actually been made, the estate finally sought $9.7 million in compensatory damages and another $1 million in damages for accounting costs it had incurred.

A jury trial began on 5 August 1992 and lasted twelve weeks. When the verdict was delivered in November, Rita was acquitted, having told the court that she'd been led astray by the other defendants. Steinberg and Zolt were found liable for three counts under the RICO anti-racketeering act, breach of their fiduciary duty, common law fraud, conversion, negligence, and gross negligence.

A few months later they were told the price they'd have to pay: $2,861,409 in compensatory damages, plus $3,029,428 in legal costs. An additional $1 million award against Steinberg in punitive damages was reduced to $250,000.

Steinberg and Zolt decided to appeal, and in December 1994 the matter went before the United States Court of Appeal for the Second Circuit.

The court documents from the appeal vividly illustrate how complex the financial shenanigans had become. In their written ruling the appeal court judges outlined the following, under the sub-heading "Facts," as the four main schemes to divert money from the estate, and also spelled out how these schemes had been concealed from the administrators.

1. Share Transfer Scheme. Before Bob Marley died he, individually, and his three wholly-owned British Virgin Islands companies (BVI Companies), received royalty payments and income from various recording and publishing contracts. The BVI Companies as personal assets of Marley would have become estate property upon his death, resulting in the estate's receipt of all of the royalty income due him. But defendants advised Rita Marley to forge her husband's signature on three documents transferring the ownership of the BVI Companies from Bob Marley to herself. The documents were pre-dated to 1978 to make it appear that Marley had made these transfers during his lifetime, thereby excluding them from estate property. Steinberg signed the documents as a witness.

Ownership of the BVI Companies was then transferred to a Netherlands Antilles company known as Music Publishing Companies of Bob Marley, N.V. (the NV or Netherlands Antilles Company), whose sole shareholder was Rita Marley. Later the BVI Companies were liquidated, their royalty-producing assets transferred to the NV Company and then, in turn, to a wholly-owned Dutch subsidiary, Bob Marley Music B.V. (the BV or Dutch Company). The result was that various amounts of royalty and other income rightfully belonging to the BVI Companies—and indirectly to the estate—were funneled between bank accounts in the names of Steinberg, the NV Company, and the BV Company and subsequently transferred into Rita Marley's personal account or into special escrow accounts set up in Zolt's name.

2. The Almo Scheme. This scheme is set forth in a letter dated December 29, 1981. It involved a signed agreement between Zolt, Steinberg, and Rita Marley not to report to the estate Bob Marley's personal share of royalty checks received from Almo Music, a music administration company for Bob Marley's song publishing activities. These royalty payments totaled about $1 million for the two years from the date of Marley's death until 1983.

3. The Island Assignment Scheme. Under this plan Rita Marley forged her late husband's signature on an assignment, again signed by Steinberg as a witness. The document, backdated to August 13, 1980, assigned Bob Marley's individual rights under contracts with Island Records to one of the BVI Companies, causing the royalties produced under those contracts to be transferred to the bank accounts of the NV Company and BV Company mentioned above, rather than to the estate.

4. The Rondor Scheme. This scheme was accomplished by assigning the assets of Tuff-Gong Productions Ltd. (Tuff-Gong Delaware), a company individually owned by Bob Marley that would have been estate property, to one of the BVI Companies. The assignment was dated as of November 30, 1980 but actually made after Bob Marley's death. It stated that the assets were transferred for the alleged consideration of $100,000, although the copyrights at issue generated millions in royalties from 1980 to 1985.

The Concealment

On December 17, 1981 letters of administration for Marley's estate were issued to co-trustees Rita Marley, Mutual Security Merchant Bank & Trust Company, a Jamaican bank, and George Desnoes, a prominent Jamaican attorney. Mutual Security, acting through George Louis Byles, its managing director, had primary responsibility for administering the estate. At a meeting to examine the estate's assets and liabilities, Steinberg told Byles that a large portion of Bob Marley's assets had been transferred to others before his death. At a later meeting on January 4, 1982 where Byles, Rita

Marley, Steinberg, and Zolt were present, Steinberg specifically indicated that the BVI Companies were not part of the estate because they had been transferred to Rita Marley before Bob Marley's death.

On June 14, 1982 Byles called another meeting in Jamaica, attended by Zolt, Steinberg, Desnoes, and Rita Marley. When Byles again inquired about the ownership of the BVI Companies, Steinberg gave him copies of the forged share transfers, dated June 6, 1978, showing that Bob Marley transferred his shares in the companies to Rita Marley before his death. Steinberg and Zolt also represented to Byles that the assets of Tuff-Gong Delaware barely exceeded that company's liabilities.

Defendants further led Byles to believe that Bob Marley had assigned his contract rights with Island Records to one of the BVI Companies. In accounting to the estate over the next six years, defendants reported only minimal amounts of royalty proceeds, failing to remit to the estate millions of dollars they had received and transferred to bank accounts of the NV Company, the BV Company, Rita Marley, Steinberg, and Zolt.

In September 1995, the appeal of Steinberg and Zolt was dismissed by the Appeal Court, one of whose judges, in a rare departure from convoluted courtroom language, had this to say: "Bob Marley was the Jamaican singer-songwriter responsible for bringing the reggae sound to the world and, to his fans, still is reggae music. Even today, fifteen years after his death from brain cancer, he continues to be the world's best-selling reggae artist. He used his music as a vehicle to spread global messages of peace, brotherhood, African unity, and international morality. For his contributions to ending political violence in Jamaica, he was awarded in 1978 the United Nations Medal of Peace. It is particularly revealing of the perversity of human nature that such a person's estate be plundered by the perfidy of his closest advisors. It is that duplicity that gave rise to the litigation before us on this appeal."

Steinberg and Zolt were not amused by the result of the appeal. But, given what might have happened to them had the Tuff Gong still been around to deal with the matter personally—

remember Don Taylor in Gabon?—they probably had much to be thankful for.

One of the first cases brought against the Marley estate was by Danny Sims, Marley's manager for several years in the early seventies. In 1984, Sims claimed that between 1973 and 1976 Bob had deliberately skirted his contractual obligations by attributing songs he had written to a variety of friends and cohorts, and in so doing had deprived Sims of millions of dollars in royalty payments that would have come to him as part of the management agreement.

Sims had a point—this time round, Bob Marley, who had been on the wrong end of rip-offs for much of his professional life, had almost certainly decided he was going to keep the songwriting royalties for himself by leading the world to believe they'd been written by trusted aides and confidants.

Unfortunately for Sims, the timing of his discovery couldn't have been worse. The Supreme Court of the State of New York ruled that the legal Statute of Limitations had run out in 1982, before the case was brought to court, and the ruling went against Sims.

Somewhat ironically, the authorship of the songs in question also figured in the most recent—at the time of writing—case involving Marley's estate. This time the central figure was Aston "Family Man" Barrett, the Wailers' formidable bass player throughout the group's Island years.

Fams, by now sixty and still touring with the Wailers, claimed that he was owed a whopping £60 million in unpaid royalties, and he had his day in court—eleven of them, between 16 March and 7 April 2006—in Britain's High Court of Justice in London.

Family Man's case was, specifically, against:
(1) Universal-Island Records Limited
(2) UMG Records Inc.
(3) Rita Marley
(4) Cedella Anita Marley
(5) David Nesta Marley
(6) Stephen Robert Nesta Marley

(7) Rohan Anthony Marley
(8) Robert Nesta Marley
(9) Karen Sophia Michelle Marley
(10) Julian Ricardo Marley
(11) Blue Mountain Music Limited
(12) Odnil Music Limited
(13) Fifty-six Hope Road Music

During the hearing, both Chris Blackwell and Rita Marley testified that Family Man had been merely a "sideman," and that, as such, he wasn't entitled to any ongoing royalties.

On 15 May, Justice Kim Lewison, Britain's leading judicial expert on contract law, gave his judgment—and it was a devastating one for the great bassman. Lewison, in a remarkably detailed ruling of more than 54,000 words, found emphatically against Fams, who was left facing legal costs of more than two million pounds.

Lewison ruled that an agreement in 1994, in which Family Man accepted a share of a settlement from the Marley estate, "compromised" the later claim. That settlement had followed two actions brought by members of the remaining Wailers in New York and Jamaica in the late 1980s.

On the basis of evidence by many of the surviving members of Bob Marley's inner circle who testified during the hearing, Lewison also concluded that Bob Marley had in fact composed virtually all of the songs that had been attributed to other people (often Family Man and Carly) during the contentious 1973–76 period: "Rebel Music (3 O'Clock Road Block)," "Talkin' Blues," "Them Belly Full (But We Hungry)," "Revolution," "War," "Want More," and "Who the Cap Fit." While acknowledging the input of several friends and Wailers band members in the songs' compositions, Lewison decreed that the essential melodies and the bulk of the lyrics had all been Bob Marley's.

Lewison, whose grasp of the history, the realities, and the subtleties of reggae's "runnings" was remarkable, alluded in his judgment to Danny Sims's earlier New York court case and concluded that: "What can, I think, be said with confidence is that it is part of Bob Marley 'lore' that writing credits on songs were given to people who played no real part in the actual composition. From what I have read and been told about Messrs Steinberg and Zolt, I find it plausible that they advised Bob Marley to deceive Danny Sims in the manner alleged. Mr. Reid Bingham came to the same conclusion when he investigated the allegation on the part of the estate. It is also, in my judgment, of significance that no songs were attributed to other writers after the end of Bob Marley's arrangements with Cayman Music; and that royalties were paid to and retained by Bob Marley or one of his companies without serious complaint by the supposed authors. Weighing all this evidence, I conclude that Bob Marley did deliberately give writing credits to people who had no part in the composition of songs with whose authorship they were credited."

The mainstream media coverage of the judgment contained little detail of Lewison's conclusions about the composition of the disputed songs, but for Marley cognoscenti these conclusions were confirmation of something they'd long suspected: that Bob Marley had written most—if not all—of the songs that had been attributed to other people.

One sad postscript to that court case is that Family Man, who played such a huge role in the success of Bob Marley and the Wailers, was expunged from the official Marley website. The man whose thundering bass defined the sound of the Wailers when they were conquering the world in the seventies is now, to all intents and purposes, a non-person in the eyes of the family of the man who had been his closest friend and musical comrade in arms.

Bunny Wailer also got in on the court action. In 1992 the only surviving member of the original Wailers brought a suit against the Marley estate for non-payment of royalties to himself and to Peter Tosh's estate. Finally, in 1999, in an out-of-court settlement, Wailer and the Tosh estate received a reported US$2 million.

The new millennium was barely started when Bunny launched a US court case against Clement "Coxson" Dodd, claiming punitive damages and royalties amounting to millions of US dollars. The suit also extended to companies acting as distributors for Dodd's massive and historic catalog, mainly the prestigious American label Heartbeat Records.

The last that was heard of that particular case was a dismissive comment by Dodd himself, who told Jamaica's *Daily Gleaner* in 2001: "It's been kicked out of the court. The suit was mainly against Heartbeat Records, but it was frivolous. The court people inspected my agreement and saw that I have the right to lease the music to whomever I choose."

In the midst of the legal wrangling, many of those who played significant roles in the story of Bob Marley and the Wailers have passed away.

The murder of Peter Tosh in September 1987 is described in some detail earlier in this book, but Peter wasn't the only Wailer to die violently that year. On 17 April—Good Friday—Carlton "Carly" Barrett, the originator of the "One Drop" style of drumming, was shot and killed as he opened the gate to his Kingston home. His wife and her boyfriend were charged with his murder but were found not guilty because of lack of evidence. He was thirty-seven.

Twelve years later, another original Wailer was also to meet a violent death in Jamaica. Junior Braithwaite, who had just returned home after living in Chicago for more than thirty years, had been attempting to revive his music career and was in the Kingston home of a fellow musician, Lawrence Scott, on the evening of 2 June 1999, when three armed men attacked them. Police said that Scott, who was also shot and killed, had been their target; Junior just happened to be in the wrong place at the wrong time. He was forty-seven.

Another legendary Jamaican musician who had played a huge role in the Wailers story also died in 1999. Joe Higgs, who had been the young Wailers' music professor in Trench Town in the sixties and had replaced Bunny on two tours in the early seventies, died on 18 December of that year in a Los Angeles hospital after battling cancer for many months. Higgs is best remembered as the Wailers' teacher and mentor, but he had a highly successful solo career, and many of his compositions reflected the tribulations and hopes of Kingston's ghetto dwellers. The most famous of them, "There's a Reward" and "So It Go," are among the finest reggae ever recorded. Higgs also composed one of Peter Tosh's best-known songs, "Stepping Razor." He was fifty-nine.

Don Taylor, the fast-talking and controversial Wailers manager, also developed health problems in the late nineties and he too passed away in 1999, in Miami, of heart complications.

Clement "Sir Coxson" Dodd spent much of the eighties and nineties in the United States, opening a popular record store and studio in Brooklyn and at the same time commuting back and forth to Kingston to keep his beloved Studio One running. On 1 May 2004, Brentford Road was renamed Studio One Boulevard, honoring Dodd for his pioneering career stretching back to the fifties. On 4 May, Dodd was working in the studio surrounded by musicians and friends when he suddenly got up and went to the bathroom. A few minutes later he was discovered sitting on a chair outside the bathroom clutching his chest and gasping for breath. Attempts to revive him failed, and he was rushed to hospital where he was pronounced dead on arrival. He was seventy-two.

Reggae music itself has often seemed in urgent need of revival. Since Bob's death in 1981, roots reggae has been all but over-whelmed by an onslaught of computerized, percussion-driven, American-influenced, endlessly repetitive, usually crude, frequently violent, often sexist, sometimes homophobic, mostly quite dreadful, and hugely popular music known, collectively, as dancehall.

Today's dancehall is often virtually indistinguishable from American rap and hip-hop, and many of today's dancehall stars collaborate and perform frequently with rap and hip-hop performers. The result amounts to cultural cloning: they all look the same, sound the same, act the same. They've got the same moves, the same two or three tired melody lines, the same scantily clad dancers "flexing" in their videos. Ironically, this musical abomination has its roots in the dancehalls of Jamaica. And, once again, Clement Dodd was in at the beginning.

The legendary Count Machuki was the man who first came up with the idea of chatting or "toasting"—as opposed to singing—

over a record. And he did it back in the fifties, the decade when ska was invented in Jamaica and the island seemed to be bursting at the seams with new musical ideas. Machuki, who was the ace DJ with Dodd's Down Beat sound system, inspired both King Stitt and U Roy to take up the new dancehall art form. As ska evolved into rock steady and then reggae, the popularity of DJs grew, with artists like I Roy, Trinity, Dillinger, and Big Youth also bursting onto the JA dancehall scene. They were so successful, in fact, that during a single week in 1970—years before the emergence of rap —U Roy held the top three places in Jamaica's pop charts (the three tracks were "Wear You to the Ball," "Wake the Town," and "Rule the Nation").

One of the stalwarts of the Jamaican dancehalls was Kool DJ Herc, the real father of modern rap and hip-hop. Herc was never a big star in Jamaica, but he played a pivotal role in the evolution of rap and hip-hop simply by leaving the island. Kingston-born Herc moved to New York in the late sixties, got himself a sound system and started carrying it to parties in the Bronx—and, in true Jamaican style, entertained the partygoers by DJ-ing over the pulsating rhythms. The "toasting" of Herc, who has been described as "the first hip-hop DJ," made a big impression on a group of aspiring young musicians who went on to call themselves Grandmaster Flash, and who were to become rap's first serious hit-makers in the mid-seventies.

Unfortunately, that music evolved over the decades into the obscenity of gangsta rap and the violent culture that came with it. Even more unfortunately, cable TV came to the islands along the way, and before long young musicians in the Caribbean were emulating the antics, lifestyles, and persona of this new breed of American performer. The dance moves became more important than the melody line. Success became synonymous with excess. The vibrations went from peaceful and positive to violent and confrontational.

Where Bob Marley and Peter Tosh had once urged people to get up, stand up for their rights, many of today's most popular Jamaican musicians are exhorting their fans to perform murder— literally. In some instances homophobia has replaced harmony, and gay people have been attacked in Jamaica as a direct result of lyrics by dancehall stars.

One love? Hardly.

In today's Jamaica, few under the age of thirty want to know about roots reggae—if it isn't dancehall, the cruder the better, they're not interested. That roots has survived at all is directly attributable to Bob Marley going "outernational" all those years ago.

Classic reggae is still enormously popular throughout the world, and roots performers continue to make a living by touring in the United States, Europe and, somewhat less frequently—only because of the distance—Africa and Asia.

And in the Caribbean, even as the surviving roots stars of the sixties and seventies near the end of their careers, there are still beacons of hope for those who prefer their music with a melody that's original, words that are uplifting, and a riddim that's deadly. The tiny Eastern Caribbean islands of St. Kitts and Dominica have produced two genuine reggae superstars, Crucial Bankie and Nasio Fontaine, who belong in the same exalted category as Burning Spear, Wailing Souls, Toots and the Maytals, the Mighty Diamonds, the Gladiators, Dennis Brown, Sugar Minnott, Steel Pulse, the Heptones, and Culture (whose magnificent lead singer, Joseph Hill, passed away while this book was being written, the biggest blow to reggae music since the death of Bob Marley. RIP, Joseph).

In Africa, where millions have come to revere Bob Marley as a god, reggae continues to flourish, with great African artists making music that matters with a distinctly African take on classic roots. Pre-eminent among them have been Alpha Blondy, Victor Essiet and the Mandators, Majek Fashek, Rocky Dawuni, and Lucky Dube, who was shot and killed in Johannesburg while this book was in its final production stages, another cruel blow to reggae. RIP, Lucky.

Many of Bob Marley's children, too, are making music that's good enough to stand up to the inevitable comparisons with their father. Ziggy and Stephen Marley, Bob's two oldest sons, were the driving force behind the immensely successful Melody Makers, with sisters Cedella and Sharon contributing harmony vocals, and have moved on to even more successful solo careers; Ky-Mani and Julian Marley have enjoyed considerable success as solo performers; and, most recently, Damian "Junior Gong" Marley, Bob's youngest son, has taken the dancehall genre to new heights with his Grammy-award-winning CD *Halfway Tree* and one of the biggest singles in the Caribbean in the new millennium, the hypnotic "Welcome to Jamrock."

But the best news of all for reggae is the world's ongoing onelove affair with Nesta Robert Marley.

Through his music and his message, Bob Marley lives.

18.

So Bob Seh

Bob Marley wasn't the easiest of interviews. Depending on the vibe, the location, the amount of ganja that had been consumed—the variables were open-ended—Bob could be difficult to pin down and, if the interviewer happened not to be Jamaican, difficult simply to understand. He could also be pointed, poetic, and eloquent, hardly surprising given his unique gift with words. In the line of duty, he made himself available for hundreds of interviews, often subjecting himself to questions that were intrusive, ignorant, rude and, occasionally, downright racist. There follow some Marley observations on everything from ganja to the Devil.

On life and his message:

"People want to listen to a message, word from Jah. This could be passed through me or anybody. I am not a leader. Messenger. The words of the songs, not the person, is what attracts people."

". . . We're born to get pressure, we come upon the earth to get pressure. You get pressure from your family, pressure from strangers, pressure from all over."

"Me have a message and me want to get it across. The message is to live. My message across the world is Rastafari. 'Righteousness shall cover the earth like water covers the sea.' Right now, no one teaching the real way of life. Right now, the Devil have plenty influence, but as far as me is concerned, all the Devil lead to is death. While Jah lead to life."

On his integrity, when questioned about his rumored involvement in horseracing scams in Jamaica:

"Me no gamble, yunno, Rasta. Man in Jamaica seh me a-win race horse. Me? I-man is a saint. My only vice is plenty woman. Other than that, I-man is a saint."

On his fame:

"Me is a natural man like any other man, and me feel like any other man. Me nuh really feel like a entertainer or a star or any o' dem t'ing deh."

On his music:

"My music defends righteousness. If you're black and you're wrong, you're wrong. It's universal. Against white people? I wouldn't say that. My music fight against the system . . . and I will keep on doing it until people have the message that Rastafari is the Almighty, and all we black people have redemption, just like anyone else. Not for money will I do anything, man, but because I have something to do. There should be no war between black and white. But until white people listen to black with open ears, there must be, well, suspicions."

On the music business:

"People rob me and try to trick me. You cyan call it trick, you call it teef. But now I have experience, now I and I see and I don't get tricked. Used to make recordings and not get royalties . . . Still happen some time. Alla dem English companies rob, man. Dem wha deal with West Indian music, pure teef dem."

On politics:

"Only one government me love—the government of Rastafari.

Politicians don't care for people, only Jah care for people. Seh, every man for himself, and God for us all. Politician cyan fall rain, dem cyan make corn, yunnerstand? The only unity we wan' get is Rasta."

On marijuana:

"Herb is the healing of the nation. There are people who live in evil and think it is right. 'Cause for instance now, a Rastaman suddun and smoke some herb, with good meditation, and a policeman come see him, stick him up, search him, beat him, and put him in prison. Now, why is this guy doing these things for? Herb just grow, like yam and cabbage. Policemen do it for evil. Dem don' wan' know God and live."

On going to Africa:

"Rastaman must go home to Africa. It sound funny to some people sometime, sometime it can sound like a mad t'ing, but our desire is fe go home to Africa. We like Jamaica, yunno, but Jamaica is spoiled as far as Rastaman is concerned. The history of Jamaica is spoiled, just like if you have an egg that break, yu cyan put it back together again. Jamaica cyan be fixed for I and I, for Rastaman. When we check out the system here, we see death. And Rastaman say, life."

"Too many people going on like only England and America are in the world. But there's a better life in Africa. I want to go there and write some music. Instead of going to New York, why can't we go to Ghana. Go to Nigeria—meet some black people, learn a new language. You see, people are only seeking material vanity. Black people are so stubborn. They stay here because white people give them a big hotel and a floor to vacuum."

"One of these days, I stop play music and I go into Africa and I don't talk to nobody no more, nor sing to nobody."

"Well I must pick a place on earth where I and I know I must live. My future is in a green part of the earth, big enough where we can roam freely. I don't think Jamaica going to be the right place, because Jamaica likkle bit small . . . the only place big enough for us is Africa."

On race:

"My father was a white and my mother black, you know. Them call me half-caste, or whatever. Well, me don't dip on nobody's side. Me don't dip on the black man's side or the white man's side. Me dip on God's side, the one who create me and cause me to come from black and white, who gave me this talent."

"What we black people cannot deal with in America, is color prejudice. You mustn't bow to the white man. You must be superior to him, that means you cannot be prejudice, because if you are superior, how can you be prejudice?"

"I don't really have no ambition. I only have one thing fe I would really like to see happen, I'd like to see mankind live together, black, white, Chinee. That's all."

On religion:

"Politics and church are the same thing . . . Dem keep the people in ignorance. These guys who preach are false."

On God's race:

"I'm sorry for the people who don't understand, 'cause they be in great tribulation when they don't have to. I would say to the people: 'Be still, and know that His Imperial Majesty, Haile Selassie I of Ethiopia, is the Almighty.' The Bible say so, Babylon newspaper say so, and I and I the children say so. So I don't see how much more reveal our people want. Wha' dem want? A white god? Well, god come black. True, true."

On the Devil:

"The Devil is a very generous man—he'll give you everything for your soul! Hear me, he's a very generous mon, a very tricky mon."

"You no want to kill the Devil—him have him part to play, him can be a good friend too. If you don't know him that's the time him can mash you down."

On money:

"Once money spoil you, boy, you ain't got no friends. You friends is your money. That mean that alla the people we have around here, them like you because you have money—and then, when your money done, you're finished."

On his white audience:

"Me no really a sing for white people me a sing for all people. The white man tek it, then the black man gwan come. So me never too are anytime I play a place and see it full up a white people. 'Caw me know seh the word go out."

On his legendary ability to be the last to bed, the first to rise:

"Sleep is an escape for fools. I must be about my Faddah's business."

On his mortality:

"Me gwan die at 36, jus' like Christ."

On poverty:

"We should all come together and create music and love, but is too much poverty. TOO MUCH POVERTY. People don't get no time to feel and spend them intelligence. The most intelligent people are the poorest people. Yes, the thief them rich, pure robbers and thieves, rich! The intelligent and innocent are poor, are crumbled and get brutalized daily. Me don't love fighting, but me don't love wicked either . . . I guess I have a kinda war thing in me. But is better to die fighting for freedom than to be a prisoner all the days of your life."

Select Bibliography

Boot, Adrian and Vivien Goldman, *Bob Marley: Soul Rebel—Natural Mystic*. Eel Pie Publishing Ltd/Hutchinson, 1981.

Boot, Adrian and Chris Salewicz, *Bob Marley: Songs of Freedom*. Bloomsbury, 1992.

Davis, Stephen, *Bob Marley: Conquering Lion of Reggae*. Plexus, 1983.

Goldman, Vivien, *The Book of Exodus: The Making & Meaning of Bob Marley & the Wailers' Album of the Century*. Random Press, 2006.

Lee-Whitney, Malika and Dermot Hussey, *Bob Marley—Reggae King of the World*. Dutton/ Pomegranate, 1984.

McCann, Ian, *Bob Marley—In His Own Words*. Omnibus Press, 1993.

McCann, Ian, *The Complete Guide to the Music of Bob Marley*. Omnibus Press, 1994.

Marley Booker, Cedella, with Anthony C. Winkler, *Bob Marley, My Son*. Taylor Trade Publishing, 1996.

Steffens, Roger, Bruce Talamon, and Leroy Jodie Pierson, *Bob Marley—Spirit Dancer*. W. W. Norton, 1994.

Steffens, Roger and Leroy Jodie Pierson, *Bob Marley and the Wailers: The Definitive Discography*. LMH Publishing, 2005.

Taylor, Don, *Marley and Me*. Kingston Publishers Ltd, 1994.

White, Timothy, *Catch a Fire—The Life of Bob Marley*. Omnibus Press, 1983.

Also recommended reading:

Davis, Stephen and Peter Simon, *Reggae Bloodlines—In Search of the Music and Culture of Jamaica*. Da Capo Press, 1997 (reprinted 1992).

Thelwell, Michael, *The Harder They Come*. Grove Press, 1980.

Index

Albums are in italics; Songs are in quotes; (p) indicates photograph

Acknowledgments

Thank you, thank you, thank you. There are so many people without whom this book would not have been possible, it should be a task worthy of the wisdom of Solomon to figure out who to acknowledge first. It isn't.

Thank you, a thousand times over, to the people of Jamaica. Without you—all of you—Bob Marley wouldn't have been, couldn't have been, who he became. Your collective spirit was part of him, and the magnitude of the debt the world owes you will only become fully apparent and fully appreciated in the centuries ahead.

To my wife, Wendy, thank you and bless you for your support in the creation of this book, from beginning to end, and for the joy you've brought into my life through your wisdom, your humor, your warmth, your kindness, your encouragement, your laughter, your patience, and especially, your love.

To David Michael Rudder: I have to tell you, I'm still at a loss for words. When I asked if you'd be willing to contribute a couple of paragraphs about what Bob Marley means to you, I had no idea you'd write a beautiful, moving poem as your personal tribute to Bob. Having the legendary "Lyrics Man" of Trinidad and Tobago alongside me on these pages is an honor I'll always treasure. Thank you, David, and walk good.

To Roger Steffens, musicologist, writer, actor, lecturer, historian, broadcaster, authority on all things Marley and all things reggae, founder and curator of the Reggae Archives in Los Angeles, and editor of the annual Bob Marley Collectors' Edition of *The Beat* magazine (phew!): thanks for your guidance, for your unstinting generosity with your remarkable collection of reggae music and reggae facts, for your tireless work on behalf of Bob's legacy and, especially, for more than two decades of friendship. The epic publication you co-authored with Leroy Jodie Pierson, *Bob Marley and the Wailers: The Definitive Discography*, was my guiding light through the maze of research that went into this book.

To the Wailers: Bob Marley always played with the best, and you guys were and are the best. More than twenty-five years after Bob left us, you're still on the road, still making great roots music, still carrying the message of Rastafari to people around the world. Bob would be more than proud.

To James Ferguson and Nicole Foster: as a professional editor, I have to tell you I couldn't have asked for more professional editors. I hope we get the chance to work together again. And the same goes for everyone else at Macmillan who helped make this book a reality—and a dream come true. Thank you.

To all those I might have inadvertently overlooked: thank you, too. And sorry about that.

One love.

—Garry Steckles, St. Kitts, West Indies